JOSÉ CLEMENT
MEXICAN MU

JOSÉ CLEMENTE
MURALISTA MEXICANO

HISTORY — LITERATURE — ART
HISTORIA — LITERATURA — ARTE

A Bilingual Study Guide
Una Guía Bilingüe de Estudios
(English — Spanish)

Spanish & Latin
American Studies
(Volume 65)

Harry E. Babbitt, Ph.D.

HARRY E BABBITT

JOSÉ CLEMENTE OROZCO MEXICAN MURALIST

JOSÉ CLEMENTE OROZCO MURALISTA MEXICANO

ISBN: 9798399671802

DEDICATION

I dedicate this book to all my former colleagues and students I've had the pleasure of working with during many years of teaching at the high school and university level. Likewise, I wish to thank my current consultants for the hard work and dedication they have shown to make this new series of bilingual guides a success.

ACKNOWLEDGMENTS

Educational Consultant (English) — Nancy Frakes, Ph.D.
Editorial Consultant (Spanish) — Mario Taglione
Technical Consultant — Oswaldo Salas
Graphic Design — Luis Ríos

TABLE OF CONTENTS

SUGGESTIONS FOR USE

This bilingual guide is for English and Spanish speakers of all ages (especially students) who wish to learn the other's language. While reading in one language, one may refer to the other version when problems or questions occur.

The life and artistic works of José Clemente Orozco in both Mexico and the United States are celebrated in both countries. Along with Diego Rivera and David Alfaro Siqueiros, Orozco is one of the three great Mexican muralists of the 20th century. In this book, we tell the story of Orozco to appreciate his importance in the history of art and politics of Mexico during a difficult time in Mexican history.

It is important to understand and remember some of the persons, places and things referred to in the chapters of ***JOSÉ CLEMENTE OROZCO, MEXICAN MURALIST***. Why not enjoy learning English or Spanish while reading and speaking about one of the most important muralists of modern times.

CHAPTER ONE
SON OF THE REVOLUTION

(01-01) José Clemente Orozco (below) who, in the future, will be one of the "three great" muralists of Mexico,[1] was born in 1883 in the State of Jalisco in the southwestern part of Mexico. To escape from a life of poverty and adversity, his family moved to Mexico City when José was very young.

(01-02) Being an extremely sensitive child, he was well aware of the hardships of that time during the last years of the dictatorship of Porfirio Díaz. Although the dictator was embellishing the capital with new buildings and beautiful avenues in the French style, the poor continued to suffer as in the past. Without doubt, José knew that sooner or later a clash between the rich and the poor was going to erupt.

(01-03) It is said that one day when José was walking to class, he noticed the cartoonist and engraver, José Guadalupe Posada, working by the window of his print shop which faced the street (next page first photo). In the future,

[1] The other two great Mexican muralists of the 20th century were Diego Rivera and David Alfaro Siqueiros.

this great artist will become famous for his satirical vignettes and drawings about Mexican life at the turn of the 20th century. By this means, he informed the public about the different events of the day with his original and amusing cartoons.

(01-04) Although Posada's funny drawings (like La Calavera Catrina, below) might have awakened in the young José's mind his first notion that art could be a powerful medium to protest certain aspects of Mexican life, at that moment he was preoccupied with other more pressing problems.

(01-05) José's parents decided their son should begin to think about choosing a profession since he was now fifteen years old. Thus, they sent him to a school to begin his studies to become an agricultural engineer. Of course, José had no interest in such a career. In a few months, he contracted rheumatic fever and returned home to recuperate. At the same time, his father was suffering from typhus and died soon thereafter, leaving Jose responsible for taking care of his mother.

(01-06) The only good result of these difficulties was that he now felt free to devote his life to the study of art, his true passion. Without losing time, he began to take art classes at the famous Academy of San Carlos (below). In order to support his mother and to pay his personal expenses, he obtained small jobs as a draftsman or designer with an architectural company.

(01-07) Now everything seemed good in his life, but very soon another tragedy befell him. The 16th of September 1904, Mexican Independence Day, was approaching. José decided to fabricate his own fireworks to celebrate that special day (below). While he was mixing the chemicals, an explosion occurred. Although he suffered severe burns, he didn't consult a doctor in time and soon his left hand had to be amputated. However, in spite of so many mishaps, José was able to continue his artistic career. In the year 1909, he decided to devote all his efforts to painting.

(01-08) The Mexican Revolution had already begun, and the country was about to suffer a decade of political and social strife in which thousands of persons would die. Between 1911 and 1916, José worked as a cartoonist at various publishing houses where he produced a series of watercolors titled *The House of Tears*, which portrayed the often sordid life in the lower class districts of Mexico City (next page first photo).

(01-09) Some art critics have compared Orozco's works of this period to those of the French artist, Toulouse-Lautrec, famous for his paintings of Parisian life in cafés, cabarets and houses of ill repute (next page second photo). In the work of both artists, one notes the compassion both had for the problems of the "street people." At the same time, José opted for critiquing Mexican society during those difficult years at the beginning of the 20th century.

« - » - « - » - « - »

BIOGRAPHICAL NOTE
JOSE GUADALUPE POSADA

José Guadalupe Posada was an extraordinary cartoonist and engraver who was born in Aguascalientes in the year 1852. After spending a time in León, Guanajuato, he moved to Mexico City in 1887 where he opened his own print shop. There he began to illustrate popular ballads which dealt with political events, terrible crimes and even predictions of the end of the world. Today, Posada is famous for his innumerable "Calaveras" (obituaries of living people) and skeletons he used to critique the evils of Mexican society during the dictatorship of Porfirio Díaz. This was his way of criticizing the rich and powerful in a humorous manner. Posada died poor, in the year 1913 after the beginning of the Mexican Revolution.

« - » - « - » - « - »

ACTIVITIES

1. Read more about José Clemente Orozco.
   https://en.wikipedia.org/wiki/Jos%C3%A9_Clemente_Orozco
2. Read about Porfirio Díaz.
   https://en.wikipedia.org/wiki/Porfirio_D%C3%ADaz
3. Read about "La Calavera Catrina".
   https://en.wikipedia.org/wiki/La_Calavera_Catrina
4. Read about the Academy of San Carlos.
   https://en.wikipedia.org/wiki/Academy_of_San_Carlos
5. Read about the Mexican Revolution.
   https://en.wikipedia.org/wiki/Mexican_Revolution
6. Read about Toulouse-Lautrec.
   https://en.wikipedia.org/wiki/Henri_de_Toulouse-Lautrec

« - » - « - » - « - »

CHAPTER ONE: QUESTIONS

1. Who were the three great Mexican muralists? (01) (Note # 1)
2. Where was (José) Orozco born? In what year? (01)
3. Why did José's family move to Mexico City? (01)
4. Who was the dictator of Mexico at that time? (02)
5. How did Porfirio Díaz embellish Mexico City? (02)
6. Who was José Guadalupe Posada? (03)
7. What did the "Calavera Catrina" represent? (04)
8. What did José's parents want their son to study? (05)
9. Why did José return home? (05)
10. Explain what happened to José's father. (05)
11. Where did José go to study art? (06)
12. How did José support his mother? (06)
13. Explain what happened to José on Mexican Independence Day in 1904. (07)
14. What did José do between 1911 and 1916? (08)
15. What did José's series of watercolors *The House of Tears* portray? (08)
16. Who was Toulouse- Lautrec? (09)
17. Explain what José's style of art was like at the beginning of the 20th century. (09)

« - » - « - » - « - »

CHAPTER TWO
OROZCO AND THE MURALIST MOVEMENT

(02-01) An important milestone in the artistic life of José Clemente Orozco occurred in the year 1922, when he joined with Diego Rivera and David Alfaro Siqueiros to initiate a muralist movement in Mexico. During the presidency of Álvaro Obregón (1920-24), José Vasconcelos (below) was named director of the Department of Public Education. He reorganized the national library and created several departments of Fine Arts and directed a program to publish works of classical authors in editions affordable for the public. Vasconcelos also brought eminent educators and artists[2] to Mexico in an attempt to improve instruction after so many years of war. One of his most important projects changed the history of art in Mexico.

[2] Among these artists were Diego Rivera, Jean Charlot, Fernando Leal, David Alfaro Siqueiros, Ramón Alva de la Canal, Fermín Revueltas. Later, José Clemente Orozco participated in the project.

(02-02) Vasconcelos convinced several outstanding painters to collaborate with him in his effort to educate the masses by means of murals painted on the walls of public buildings like the "Old Colegio de San Ildefonso." This edifice in the historic center of Mexico City had once been the residence of Jesuit students and then had become the National Preparatory School. At last, in 1992, it was converted into one of the most important museums in the Mexican capital (below).

(02-03) It was here where several artists painted murals with Mexican themes, especially the Revolution. Thus, little by little, a nationalistic, didactic and popular movement arose to put into practice the concept of "street art" with a clearly leftist ideology. José Clemente Orozco participated in this movement headed by Vasconcelos by painting some frescos on the north walls of the three levels of the principal patio, using the Mexican Revolution as his theme.

(02-04) Orozco's first murals may be seen in the "Old Colegio de San Ildefonso" where the young José had studied years previously. A copy of the fresco is called *Maternity* and is the only image of a work remaining from the original part of the project in the said "Colegio" (below). Some say that it shows the great influence of European Renaissance art, perhaps that of Botticelli.

(02-05) At that time, many people criticized the work because he had painted a nude Virgin with Child. However, Orozco declared it was not his intention to paint a virgin, but only a mother (next page first photo). Finally, Orozco himself decided to destroy the work in order to have a room to paint one of his murals that we see today in the exact same place.

(02-06) Another of Orozco's murals in the "Old Colegio de San Ildefonso" is a work titled *Hernán Cortés and Malinche* (next page second photo). She was a young Indian girl who became the "conquistador's" mistress. At their feet lies the young son they had together. (See History Note) The three figures are nude, some-what similar to Adam and Eve. Some say that their offspring perhaps represents a battered and degenerate nation caused by the mixture of races. One can denote the contrast between the whiteness of Cortés and the traditional dark Indian color of Malinche. It is not clear whether Cortés is displaying a protective or dominating gesture toward

Malinche. However, it is evident Orozco paints her as Mexico's mother, but we do not know if he believes that this is good or bad.

(02-07) Also at the "Old Colegio de San Ildefonso", Orozco painted some scenes, perhaps explaining some of the causes of the Mexican Revolution, one of which was the breach between the rich and the poor. The mural below titled *Banquet of the Rich* shows the great discontent of the lower class at that time.

(02-08) In the upper part of the mural we see the banquet of the rich people, well dressed, enjoying a good meal and having a good time at the expense of the poor (next page first photo). Orozco uses brilliant colors to point out important objects and persons. The orange background suggests a fire and emphasizes the intensity of the atmosphere or the relations between the rich and impoverished masses. The tone in general reflects the hostile interaction between the two groups.

(02-09) In the lower part of the same work, we see three men with their everyday tools who represent the working class in their daily struggle to survive in a country governed by the elite class. The finger of a rich man points out the hammer, which is one of the symbols of communism (next page second photo). We remember that the Russian

Revolution began in 1917 at the same time that the poor in Mexico were fighting a government that was exploiting them.

« - » - « - » - « - »

HISTORY NOTE #1
MALINCHE — DOÑA MARINA

Malinche, (next page) also known by the name of Doña Marina, was one of the twenty slaves given as tribute to Hernán Cortés when he defeated the Indian warriors in the region of Tabasco in the year 1519. Malinche spoke the language of the Aztecs and also that of the Mayas. She learned Castilian and served the Spaniards as an interpreter during the conquest of Mexico. Furthermore, Doña Marina informed the Spaniards about the social and military customs of the natives of Mexico. One of the conquerors once said that "after God, the major reason for the success of the conquest of Mexico was Doña Marina." Today, everyone knows that Doña Marina became Cortés' mistress. After the conquest of Tenochtitlán in 1521, she gave birth to a son with Cortés called Martin, who would be one of the first "mestizos" (persons of mixed blood) born in Mexico.

Today in Mexico, the word "malinchismo" refers to persons who prefer a style of life different from their own culture or a life with foreign influences. Some Mexicans believe Malinche betrayed the indigenous peoples by supporting the Spaniards in the conquest of Mexico. On the other hand, some see her as the founding figure of the Mexican nation. In recent years, Doña Marina has been converted into a half mythical and half-legendary figure. Her life has been the theme of many movies and literary works.

« - » - « - » - « - »

HISTORY NOTE #2
THE MEXICAN "CORRIDO"

The Mexican "corrido" is a popular narrative in the form of a song, poetry or ballad (below). Before the popularity of radio and television and the electronic media, the "corrido" was used to inform and educate the public, especially the lower class, about the events that were occurring in the country, such as the Mexican Revolution. Many "corridos" celebrated the deeds of heroes like Pancho Villa and Emiliano Zapata. The popularity of the "corridos" was due to their simple language and pleasing music. Some of the favorite "corridos" of that epoch were *La Cucaracha*, *Adelita* and *La Valentina*.

At present, the "corridos" have developed a great deal and are dedicated to the memory of important events and famous persons during a period that has now passed into history. Below we quote the "corrido" of Gabino Palomares (next page) called *The Curse of Malinche*, which can be heard on YouTube.

« - » - « - » - « - »

HISTORY NOTE #3
LA CUCARACHA — THE COCKROACH

Without doubt, the most famous "corrido" of the Mexican Revolution is "La Cucaracha." The song is recognized almost everywhere in the world. It deals with a cockroach that has lost one of its six legs and attempts to walk using the five that remain. The song's words and rhythm imitate the irregular gait that the cockroach uses in order to walk.

It is said that the Mexican soldiers sang "corridos"' like this one during their long marches through the deserts and mountains of Mexico. There are dozens of different versions of the words that vary according to the political whims of the moment and place. Some say that the lyrics refer to Pancho Villa because his long arms and legs stuck out of the Model-T Ford he used. On another occasion it makes allusions to Victoriano Huerta because it is said that he smoked marihuana. At any rate, the song makes fun of and ridicules everyone.

« - » - « - » - « - »

ACTIVITIES

1. Read about Diego Rivera.
   https://en.wikipedia.org/wiki/Diego_Rivera
2. Read about David Alfaro Siqueiros.
   https://en.wikipedia.org/wiki/David_Alfaro_Siqueiros
3. Read about José Vasconcelos.
   https://en.wikipedia.org/wiki/Jos%C3%A9_Vasconcelos
4. Read about the "Colegio de San Ildefonso".
   https://en.wikipedia.org/wiki/San_Ildefonso_College
5. Read about the Mexican "Corrido".
   https://en.wikipedia.org/wiki/Corrido
6. Listen to the "corrido" called *The Curse of Malinche*.
   https://www.youtube.com/watch?v=vEVQiw7ROog
7. Listen to the "corrido" called *Adelita.*
   https://www.youtube.com/watch?v=EoR1dyGhGt8

« - » - « - » - « - »

CHAPTER TWO: QUESTIONS

1. What milestone did José achieve in the year 1922? (01)
2. Who was José Vasconcelos? Describe his achievements. (01)
3. Who collaborated with José Vasconcelos? For what purpose? (02)
4. What occurred in the year 1922? (02)
5. What was the theme of the so-called "street art"? (03)
6. Describe Orozco's fresco called *Maternity.* (04)
7. Why did some critics criticize the painting *Maternity*? (05)
8. Who was Malinche? (06) (History Note # 1)
9. Describe what some say about the painting *Hernán Cortés and Malinche.* (06)

10. What is the title of one of Orozco's murals about the Mexican Revolution? (07)
11. Describe Orozco's mural titled *Banquet of the Rich*. (08)
12. What does the hammer represent? (09)
13. In what year did the Russian Revolution begin? (09)

« - » - « - » - « - »

CHAPTER THREE
OROZCO'S MURAL AT POMONA COLLEGE

(03-01) In the year 1928, Orozco began the second chapter of his artistic life with a trip to the United States. There he opened an exposition of his *Drawings of the Revolution,* which had a notable success and thus José was able to cover the cost of his basic necessities. A short time later, he received a commission to paint a mural at Pomona College in Claremont, California. It was here, in the dining room of Frary Hall, where Orozco was the first of the "three great" Mexican painters to paint a mural in the United States. José arrived at Claremont in March 1930 and worked for three months painting a mural called *Prometheus,* which can be seen at the back of the dining room (below).

(03-02) Before commenting on the significance of this work by Orozco, we should speak briefly about Prometheus. By reviewing a little of this interesting story, we can better understand the important message of this mural.

(03-03) *In Greek mythology Prometheus was one of the Titans (a group of powerful deities), descendants of Gaia (The*

Earth) and Uranus (Sky) who ruled during Greece's Golden Age. One of the Greek myths tells how Prometheus deceived Zeus (god of the sky and king of the gods of Mount Olympus). It is told that Prometheus prepared a sacrifice to Zeus and divided it into two parts. One part contained the entrails and the meat. In the other part, Prometheus placed the bones covered with a tasty gravy. Then he asked Zeus to choose the part he preferred. Zeus chose the part that had the gravy, thinking that it would be more appetizing.

(03-04) *When Zeus heated the part he had chosen, he discovered it was nothing but bones. Zeus became furious and took fire away from Man. In a short time, Prometheus ascended Mount Olympus and stole fire out of the chariot of Helios who, according to another myth, bore the sun through the sky every day in said chariot. Zeus shows his fury again when he ordered Hephaestus (god of the sun and the forge) to create a woman out of clay to be named Pandora. Some time later, Zeus sent Pandora to the house of Prometheus' brother. The latter had in his house a locked box where he kept all the evils in the world like the worst plagues and diseases* (next page first photo). *When Pandora arrived at the brother's house, she found the box and opened it, thus exposing humanity to all these abominations. Who has not heard of Pandora's famous box?*

(03-05) *For the Greeks, Prometheus was important because he believed he had given the gift of fire to Man so that all might benefit from light and progress in the form of the arts, sciences and civilization in general.*

(03-06) Orozco painted the gigantic figure of Prometheus, who dominates the entire mural. The red flames illuminate the Titan's body. At the moment of snatching the sun to bring it down to Earth, his hands seem to meld into the flames as in an abstract cubist painting. On either side of Prometheus, there are groups of earthly mortals writhing in different states of torment and anguish (next page).

(03-07) The detail in the next page represents the moment in which Prometheus delivers fire to human beings. Humanity has suffered oppression, and now, with the gift of the Titan before them, there are diverse reactions. Some seem to be terrorized, while others demonstrate their enthusiasm.

(03-08) Perhaps the lesson for human beings, today as in centuries past, is to know how to take advantage to the fullest the gifts we have received. These come in the form of intelligence that we can use to emerge from obscurity and improve our lives. At the same time, Mankind must be careful because the same flame that purifies can also burn and destroy all that it touches. The moral of this mural gives it a universal appeal for all times.

« - » - « - » - « - »

ACTIVITIES

1. Read more about Prometheus.
   https://en.wikipedia.org/wiki/Prometheus
2. Read more about Pandora's Box.
   https://en.wikipedia.org/wiki/Pandora%27s_box

« - » - « - » - « - »

CHAPTER THREE: QUESTIONS

1. In what year did Orozco arrive in the United States? (01)
2. What was Orozco's opening exposition called? (01)

3. Where did Orozco receive a commission to paint a mural? (01)
4. What was the name of Orozco's first mural? (01)
5. How long did it take Orozco to paint his first mural? (01)
6. Who was Prometheus? (03)
7. Describe the sacrifice that Prometheus prepared to Zeus. (03)
8. What part did Zeus choose and what was the result? (03) (04)
9. What did Prometheus steal from Helios' chariot? (04)
10. How did Zeus show his fury again? (04)
11. Who was Pandora? (04)
12. What did Prometheus' brother have locked in a box? (04)
13. Why was Prometheus important to the Greeks? (05)
14. Describe Orozco's mural of Prometheus. (06)
15. Describe the moment when Prometheus delivers fire to human beings. (07)
16. What is the moral of Orozco's mural for Mankind? (08)

« - » - « - » - « - »

CHAPTER FOUR
OROZCO'S MURALS AT DARTMOUTH COLLEGE

(04-01) Between 1932 and 1934, Orozco painted a series of murals called *The Epic of American Civilization* in the Baker Library at Dartmouth College in Hanover, New Hampshire. As a theme, he chose the impact that the clash of different cultures, both native and European, had on the North American continent. As a point of departure in the study of this topic, we should be aware that Dartmouth College (below) was founded in the year 1769 to provide instruction to native Americans. In their classes, the white teachers taught the basic ideas about Western Culture. In this way, they tried to phase out the use of the indigenous languages and beliefs. As the centuries passed, Dartmouth College became one of the most prestigious higher educational institutions in the United States, but the Indians have all but disappeared.

(04-02) Orozco worked almost two years in order to complete a series of twenty-four murals which cover different aspects of the interesting history of some of the indigenous civilizations of North America and how they influenced the life of the colonists and future events in the development of the "American" civilization of today. We are going to briefly analyze some of the most significant panels (below). The first ten deal with the migration of the Indians to North America. At first, the newly arrived natives were alone, and many were frightened. Thus, they created gods and offered them human sacrifices in exchange for their protection and benevolence.

(04-03) In another panel (next page) we see a place divided between the spiritual and physical world. Quetzalcóatl,[3] the mythical white god of the Toltecs, has arrived and is disinterring the ancient gods who are wearing curious masks. He is the "Civilizing God" and "Teacher of Men" who, according to tradition, is initiating a new epoch in which he teaches the native peoples the basic elements of agriculture and the arts. As a result of his teachings, the people have built magnificent pyramids and civilization continues to progress for many centuries until reaching a Golden Age for the indigenous peoples of that epoch.

---

[3] Quetzalcóatl — The "Plumed Serpent."

(04-04) One of the many legends tells us that Quetzalcóatl is opposed to the human sacrifices so popular among the older gods. To seek revenge, Quetzalcóatl's enemies play a joke on him and he becomes drunk and causes a woman to lose her honor. Ashamed of such an act and convinced that he can do no more for his people, Quezalcóatl goes to the coast along the Gulf of Mexico. There he is converted into the "Morning Star" and takes leave of his subjects. Before departing, he promises to return to his people on a certain date, which coincides with the arrival of the Spaniards in the year 1519. Upon seeing Cortés, many natives naturally believe that Quetzalcóatl, their blessed white god, has returned.

(04-05) In the next page, we see Cortés standing beside the cross. The predominant color is black, symbolizing the death of the beautiful indigenous civilization of Mexico. It is replaced by the machines seen on the right side of the mural. For Orozco, these represent the beginning of the "Age of Technology" which many enjoy today.

(04-06) As we proceed to another panel, we note the various differences between Anglo-Saxon America to the left (next page first photo) and Hispanic America to the right. The principal personage in Anglo-Saxon[4] America is the teacher with her Bible. Her compatriots seem to be enjoying peace, money, and order. For Orozco, everyone is cut from the same mold. The children and the old men dress alike in various tones of gray. On the other hand, the principal personage of Hispanic America is a humble soldier of the Mexican Revolution. He is surrounded by corrupt politicians and generals who have brought war, destruction, poverty, misery and death to the homeland.

(04-07) In the mural titled *Gods of the Modern World*, Orozco strongly criticizes the educational system in the United States (next page second photo). In the background, we see several professors who take the form of skeletons or mummies wearing their traditional tunics and caps. Further down, we notice a feminine skeleton (shows the influence of

---

[4] Anglo-Saxon — The Anglo-Saxons were migrants from northern Europe who settled in England in the fifth and sixth centuries. Initially comprising many small groups and divided into a number of kingdoms, the Anglo-Saxons were finally joined into a single political realm — the kingdom of England.

the caricaturist, José Guadalupe Posada) that is giving birth to a dead embryo similar to the others we see in their small glass coffins. For Orozco, these lifeless fetuses are symbols of the useless knowledge contained in the dark, almost black, books at the mother's side.

(04-08) Many art critics have pointed out that it is ironic that Orozco was invited to paint a mural in the library at Dartmouth College, which was founded precisely to convert the Indians to the religion and customs of the Anglo-Saxons of New England. Today Dartmouth College is a center of technology and learning that represents all the "evils" that Orozco painted in his murals, which students pass daily on their way to class.

(04-09) The remaining panels of Orozco's frescos at Dartmouth allude to modern civilization as a threat to the survival of the indigenous races of North America. In the United States, little remains of that ancient culture, especially in New England[5]. On the other hand, in Mexico, several million Indians still live and continue speaking over fifty native languages. Although some now communicate on their cell phones and watch soap operas on television, they have been able to conserve many of their customs of the past (below).

« - » - « - » - « - »

[5] New England — a territory in the northeastern part of the United States which includes six states: Maine, New Hampshire, Vermont, Massachusetts, Connecticut and Rhode Island.

ACTIVITIES

1. Read about Quetzalcóatl. https://en.wikipedia.org/wiki/Quetzalcoatl

« - » - « - » - « - »

CHAPTER FOUR: QUESTIONS

1. Where did Orozco paint his second series of frescoes in the United States? (01)
2. What theme did Orozco choose for this series of frescoes? (01)
3. In what year was Dartmouth College founded? For what purpose? (01)
4. Explain the subject matter of the first ten of the series of twenty-four murals. (02)
5. Who was Quetzalcóatl? (03)
6. What did Quetzalcóatl teach his people? (03)
7. What was the consequence of the joke of the enemies of Quetzalcóatl? (04)
8. Before departing, what did Quetzalcóatl promise to do? (04)
9. What occurred in the year 1519? (04)
10. Describe how Cortés appears in the mural. (05)
11. What do the machines represent in this mural? (05)
12. Who were the Anglo-Saxons? (06) (Note # 2)
13. Describe how Orozco portrays Anglo-Saxon America in this mural. (06)
14. Describe how Orozco portrays Hispanic America in the same mural. (06)
15. Describe the mural titled *Gods of the Modern World*. (07)
16. What influence is evident in this mural? (07)
17. What irony have some critics pointed out? (08)
18. Describe what Dartmouth College teaches today. (08)
19. What do the remaining panels refer to? (09)

20. Explain how the United States differs from Mexico in the life of the indigenous peoples. (09)

« - » - « - » - « - »

CHAPTER FIVE
OROZCO AT THE UNIVERSITY OF GUADALAJARA

(05-01) After finishing his well-received murals at Pomona and Dartmouth Colleges, Orozco returns to Mexico. He decides to accept the invitation of the governor of the state of Jalisco to paint murals in three of the most prominent institutions in Guadalajara — the University of Guadalajara, the Jalisco State Government Palace and the Hospicio Cabañas. Orozco will dedicate five years of his life, creating what will be considered his crowning masterpieces. Below we see the façade of the University that today is a museum.

(05-02) One of Orozco's murals at the university is painted on the stage in the auditorium where the university officials hold their meetings. The mural is called *The People and Their False Leaders*. Here Orozco is critical of the monopoly of education by the rich and privileged class. This occurred during the reign of the dictatorship of Porfirio Díaz that lasted for approximately thirty years and ended in 1911. Below is Diego Rivera's rendition of Porfirio Díaz (center), his wife and José Limantour, finance minister of Mexico.

(05-03) Orozco's mural shows the great disparity between the rich, the so-called "company men" or owners of the large "haciendas" (country state) and the poor uneducated masses (next page first photo). On the left are the "company men" with their guns and clubs who rule the lives of the masses who cultivate the fields. The general at the top seems to be observing the stand-off below. We notice in the lower part of this detail that the rich are the only ones with books. The characters on the right seem to be giving a lecture or sermon to the poor, while one man points to them with a sword. This struggle eventually led to the Mexican Revolution that lasted approximately ten years (1910-1920).

(05-04) On the right side of the mural (next page second photo), the workers show signs of hunger or even starvation. The different facial expressions show the anger and contempt they have for their masters. The oppressors seem to point to their books to justify their repression of the workers. The flames between the two sides perhaps suggest the bloody revolution that is about to explode when the authoritarians will be swallowed up in flames.

(05-05) As we peer up at the dome of the auditorium, we see another of Orozco's beautiful murals called *The Creative and Rebellious Man* (below). The first thing we notice is the great contrast between the characters in the previous mural and those in this dome. Orozco has painted four male human figures, three of them ascending. These, no doubt, symbolize teaching, technique and science. Three of the men represented are naked and may represent physical, moral, intellectual, and spiritual purity. At the top, the hanged man is probably being punished for his rebellion. At the bottom we see a two-headed pentaphasic[6] man who represents science with its branches.

[6] Pentaphasic — probably refers to five (penta) branches of science.

(05-06) Now let's separate the mural and look at each of the four men and consider what each may represent. At the same time, we must not forget that there are various interpretations of each part of this mural. We begin with a close-up of the so-called "pentaphasic" man — perhaps a wise man or scientist (below). Each of those five heads or faces is perhaps a manifestation of the one person. He appears to be naked and is surrounded by several elements that suggest a variety of functions. In his right hand, he holds a scale meter and in his left hand a compass. One face seems to be looking at geometric lines and projections drawn in white. At the tip of the compass, we observe some anatomical parts such as a heart and digestive system. The small figure in black at the bottom seems to be a body with a trepanned skull, perhaps representing medicine. Under his left hand are some sheets of paper that might evoke literature and laws.

(05-07) The second man may be a laborer or working man (next page). He seems to grip the controls of a powerful futuristic metal machine which he controls with his right hand. This man seems to be proud of his work. One critic has observed that the fusion of his hand with the head of the rebel might suggest that he is waiting for the appropriate moment to join him through an act of rebellion.

(05-08) The man in the next page first photo we might call the "rebel". In the mural he seems to be falling, but here we have turned him upside down for a better look. This man who has been hanged seems to be a mystical being. His forearm is covered with a red cloak. Since the hand of the worker (as mentioned previously) seems to join the head of the rebel, this may be a way of transmitting knowledge.

(05-09) In contrast with the "rebel", we see a man neatly dressed in white, which here seems to have a special meaning (next page second photo). In ancient Rome, office-seekers wore a gleaming white toga, presumably to indicate the purity of their intentions when seeking a role in civic affairs. The man in white, next page second photo, is the candidate[7] who is going to change the condition. In this case, we must

[7] Candidate — Notice the interesting etymology of the word. It means "shining white" like the togas worn by the Romans who were seeking office.

consider what "condition" Orozco is referring to. Most likely, it is the stark contrast between the rich and the poor during the Mexican Revolution. The function of this man in white is that of a teacher. He raises his right arm toward the "rebel" and points to him with his index finger. Perhaps this teacher can be the inspiration for change in Mexico in the future.

« - » - « - » - « - »

ACTIVITIES

1. Read more about the Mexican revolution.
   https://en.wikipedia.org/wiki/Mexican_Revolution
2. Read more about the Government Palace in Guadalajara. (Spanish only)
   https://es.wikipedia.org/wiki/Palacio_de_Gobierno_de_Jalisco

« - » - « - » - « - »

CHAPTER FIVE: QUESTIONS

1. After returning to Mexico, where did Orozco go to paint? (01)
2. How many years of his life did Orozco dedicate to painting his masterpieces? (01)
3. Describe Orozco's mural titled *The People and Their False Leaders.* (02)
4. Who was Porfirio Díaz? (02)
5. Who was José Limantour? (02)
6. What is an "hacienda"? (03)
7. Describe the "company men". (03)
8. What led up to the Mexican Revolution? How long did it last? (03)
9. Describe the right side of the mural. (04)
10. Describe the mural called *The Creative and Rebellious Man*. (05)
11. Who might the "pentaphasic man" be? (06)
12. To whom might the five heads or faces belong? (06)
13. What does this man hold in his right hand? In his left hand? (06)
14. What is one of his faces looking at? (06)
15. What do we see at the tip of his compass? (06)
16. Describe the figure in black. (06)
17. What do we see under his left hand? (06)
18. Describe the laborer. (07)

19. What has one critic observed? (07)
20. Describe the "rebel". (08)
21. What may be the "rebel's" way of transmitting knowledge? (08)
22. What does the "man in white" represent? (09)
23. What might be the function of the "man in white"? (09)
24. What may be his relationship with the "rebel"? (09)

« - » - « - » - « - »

CHAPTER SIX
OROZCO IN THE GOVERNMENT PALACE

(06-01) In the year 1948, Orozco began his last monumental work in the Government Palace in the Plaza de Armas of Guadalajara. This beautiful building dates from the year 1790. Its baroque style, perhaps a little severe, gives the structure a feeling of noble austerity (below).

(06-02) The elegant columns and beautiful rounded arches in the interior patio (next page first photo) are jewels of civil architecture of the 18th century. Around the spacious corridors there are different salons where the visitor can learn about the history of Guadalajara, capital of the State of Jalisco.

(06-03) In this building, Father Hidalgo signed the decree abolishing slavery on December 6, 1810. Orozco portrays Hidalgo surrounded by slaves in chains (next page second photo).

LIBERTAD
REFORMA

(06-04) In the lower part (below) we see some of the leaders of the so-called "Reform Laws of 1857," headed by Benito Juárez (wearing the red necktie with the colors of Mexico) who will become president of Mexico over forty years later.

(06-05) Perhaps the most impressive mural that Orozco painted in the Government Palace at the head of the principal stairway is his emotional tribute to Father Hidalgo. He is seen in vivid colors boldly grasping his lighted torch while he raises his left fist as a symbol of strength. There is no doubt that he is dedicated to the defense of his political ideals (next page first photo).

(06-06) At the feet of Father Hidalgo, we observe the battles fought against the dark forces that have always exploited the poor (next page second photo). The enemies of the poor and downtrodden fall into the flames of hell.

(06-07) Orozco uses tones of gray and black to give emphasis to his theme. Many daggers are needed to eliminate the evildoers of Mexico (next page first photo).

(06-08) In contrast, another image of Hidalgo is shown in the Assembly Hall of the Legislative Branch. He is less exalted and even sad. It is said that it was the last mural work painted by Orozco. It is called *The Contemporary Circus (below)*.

(06-09) Orozco also includes other forces that do damage to society and their symbols like the cross, swastika and the hammer and sickle (below). Here, Orozco does not promote anyone's political ideology.

(06-10) Orozco uses red to emphasize the evil of Hitler and the red flag and hammer and sickle of communism.

« - » - « - » - « - »

ACTIVITIES

1. Read more about the Government Palace in Guadalajara. (Spanish only) https://es.wikipedia.org/wiki/Palacio_de_Gobierno_de_Jalisco
2. Read more about Father Hidalgo. https://en.wikipedia.org/wiki/Miguel_Hidalgo_y_Costilla
3. Read about Benito Juárez. https://en.wikipedia.org/wiki/Benito_Ju%C3%A1rez

« - » - « - » - « - »

CHAPTER SIX: QUESTIONS

1. Describe the Government Palace. (01) (02)
2. When was slavery abolished in Mexico? Who signed the decree? (03)
3. Who was the leader of the so-called "Reform Laws" of Mexico? (04)
4. Describe the most impressive mural in the Government Palace. (05)
5. Whom do we see at the feet of Father Hidalgo? (06)
6. Describe the appearance of these people. (07)
7. What was the last mural painted by Orozco? (08)
8. What are some of the symbols used in this painting? What do they symbolize? (09) (10)

CHAPTER SEVEN
OROZCO IN THE "HOSPICIO CABAÑAS"

(Part One)

(07-01) During the years 1938 and 1939, Orozco painted fifty-three frescos in the current Cabañas Cultural Institute in the city of Guadalajara (below). This historic building was constructed at the beginning of the 19th century by Bishop Juan Cruz Ruiz de Cabañas. He chose the famous architect, Manuel Tolsá, to make the designs for what would be known in the future as the "Hospicio (Orphanage) Cabañas" until the year 1980. This huge building has 23 patios, 106 rooms and 465 arches.

(07-02) Here, the bishop successfully established a workshop for orphans and a refuge for the old and disabled. In the next page first photo, we see some children playing in the street in front of the building in 1920.

(07-03) Since the orphanage contains some of Orozco's most famous frescos, it was converted into a center for art and culture under the name "Cabañas Cultural Institute." Finally, in the year 1997, UNESCO declared it to be a World Heritage Site. As Orozco began to paint the murals on its walls and ceiling, he attempted to show both the positive and negative aspects of Mexico's two cultures — the indigenous and the Spanish (below second photo).

(07-04) In the detail below, Philip II of Spain is carrying a cross and a crown, symbolizing the arrival of the Spaniards in the New World.

(07-05) Orozco painted the images of two famous Spaniards — the writer Miguel Cervantes (left) and the famous painter El Greco. They are seated on a wall that culminates in an arch with a window between them (below).

(07-06) Both are dressed as men of distinction. Below we see a close-up of Cervantes, author of the famous novel *Don Quijote*, some say the most read novel of all time.

(07-07) El Greco (below) was one of the most notable painters of Spain. Orozco shows that each of these two figures is representative of a cultural rupture that each made in his time.

(07-08) Orozco painted one of the first caravels or ships that brought Columbus and other early explorers to the New World (below). Columbus believed he had arrived in the East Indies where he would find the spices that were in much demand in Europe. For this reason, he called the native people Indians.

(07-09) The scene of a "conquistador" astride a two-headed horse represents the conquest of Mexico (next page first photo). Tenochtitlán, the Aztec capital (now Mexico City) fell to the Spaniards in 1521. Horses played an important role in the conquest since the Indians had never seen this type of animal before. At first, the natives believed that the rider and the horse were one animal. The Spaniards used them as a form of transportation and while mounted, they were able to kill many Indians.

(07-10) According to Orozco, the Indians saw horses as animals with heads of metal. At their feet lie some of the many indigenous victims of this strange animal (next page second photo).

« - » - « - » - « - »

ACTIVITIES

1. Read about Bishop Juan Cruz Ruiz de Cabañas. (Only Spanish)

https://es.wikipedia.org/wiki/Juan_Cruz_Ruiz_de_Cabañas%C3%B1as

2. Read about the Cabañas Cultural Institute. https://en.wikipedia.org/wiki/Hospicio_Caba%C3%B1as
3. Read about Miguel de Cervantes. https://en.wikipedia.org/wiki/Miguel_de_Cervantes
4. Read about El Greco. https://en.wikipedia.org/wiki/El_Greco

« - » - « - » - « - »

CHAPTER SEVEN: QUESTIONS

1. How many frescos did Orozco paint in the Cabañas Cultural Institute? (01)
2. Who constructed this historic building? (01)
3. What architect did he choose for the design? (01)
4. Until what year did this building serve as an orphanage? (01)
5. Describe this building. (01)
6. For what purpose did this building serve? (02)
7. What occurred in the year 1997? (03)
8. What did Orozco try to show in his murals? (03)
9. Describe how Orozco portrays King Philip II. (04)
10. What two famous Spaniards did Orozco paint? (05)
11. Describe how Orozco placed these two Spaniards in the mural. (05)
12. What famous novel did Cervantes write? (06)
13. Who is one of the most notable painters of Spain? (07)
14. What type of ship was used to carry Columbus to the New World? (08)
15. Why did Columbus try to find a new route to the East Indies? (08)
16. What was the importance of horses in the New World? (09)
17. What was the name of the Aztec capital? (09)

18. Why, perhaps, does Orozco paint a two-headed horse? (09)
19. How did the Indians see horses at that time? (10)

« - » - « - » - « - »

CHAPTER EIGHT
OROZCO IN THE "HOSPICIO CABAÑAS"

(Part Two)

(08-01) After arriving in New Spain (Mexico), the Spaniards were horrified by the human sacrifices carried out by the Indians. With dynamic figures and images, Orozco painted these primitive and bloody rituals practiced by the pre-Hispanic cultures (below).

(08-02) The theme of the mural (next page first photo) is the armed conquest as a symbol of violence. Here we see Cortés as a machine. His body is held together with nuts, bolts and screws. In the upper part of the mural, Cortés seems to have his mechanical arm shielding the priest. Even his sword appears to be an extension of his body. At his feet are the mutilated bodies of Indians. As a result, Cortés' sword is stained with the blood of the indigenous race.

C

(08-03) As we view the mural upside down, we can better see the portrait of the priest. Perhaps this is Orozco's way of portraying both as complicit in the subjugation and death of so many of the native race (below).

(08-04) On the other hand, Orozco portrayed the Christian charity that the Spaniards brought to the New World. A priest prays for the soul of a recent victim that lies at his feet.

(08-05) Orozco also critiques the great struggles and conflicts that caused the death of so many Spaniards as well as Indians (below).

(08-06) In another mural at the Hospicio Cabañas, Orozco shows how the priests tried to convert the Indians to Catholicism and teach them different trades. In fact, after the conquest, different Catholic Orders built hundreds of convents to teach the Indians the Spanish language (Notice the letters ABCD). The knotted cord worn by the priest below indicates he is of the Franciscan Order. Since the point of the cross looks more like a dagger, perhaps Orozco is implying that the conversions were not always done with the free will of the Indians.

(08-07) The wheel, unknown by the indigenous peoples of the New World, symbolizes the advances of western civilization that later gave rise to mechanization in Mexican society at that time (next page first photo).

(08-08) According to Orozco, as new inventions like the wheel change the world, people tend to forget the traditions and customs of their ancestors. Below we see the wheel has perhaps crushed the old poets and philosophers of centuries past.

(08-09) The painter also shows the contrast between the first rudiments of science introduced by Europeans and the superstitions of the indigenous cultures of Mexico (below, right).

(08-10) In the detail in the next page first photo, Orozco paints the demagogues, dressed in black, who are found at all levels of Mexican society.

(08-11) Another painting shows a group of despots who appear with different faces in all colors (next page second photo).

(08-12) In another archway, Orozco painted a statue of the beloved Bishop Juan Cruz de Cabañas who, so many years ago, founded the orphanage for poor abandoned children and the homeless elders of Guadalajara (below).

(08-13) Many critics say that the high point of Orozco's art is his fresco called *Man in Flames* (next page), which can be seen in the dome of the "Hospicio Cabañas." It is approximately thirty-three feet in diameter and eighty feet high. This gigantic circular mural is surrounded by another sixteen smaller frescos with different themes related to the *Man in Flames*.

(08-14) In the circular mural we can distinguish four persons — one figure in the center and three others intertwined around the first. There are various interpretations of the meaning of this masterpiece. For some, the mural represents the world of the indigenous cultures and their barbarous human sacrifices. The figure in the center may be the person sacrificed by the other three persons who surround him (next page first photo). Perhaps the man in the lower part is the priest in charge of carrying out the sacrifice. Thus, the color red not only represents the flames, but also the victim's blood. Others suggest that the figures in the mural represent the four elements of nature — fire, air, water and earth. Another possible interpretation is that the figure in the center is perhaps Christ who is being sacrificed for the sins of Man. It may be that the smaller images around the four persons represent such sins as war, slavery, cruelty and other evils of modern society.

(08-15) Other critics maintain that the main figure in the fresco represents Prometheus, the god who gave fire to humanity (next page second photo). The man under him may be Zeus. It is ironic that Prometheus is being consumed by the same fire that he gave mankind. The most important effect of the mural is that it makes us think. It is not necessary to have a single meaning in mind in order to appreciate this magnificent work of Orozco.

« - » - « - » - « - »

ACTIVITIES

1. Read about Prometheus.
   https://en.wikipedia.org/wiki/Prometheus
2. Read about Zeus.
   https://en.wikipedia.org/wiki/Zeus

« - » - « - » - « - »

CHAPTER EIGHT: QUESTIONS

1. What country today is New Spain? (01)
2. What horrified the Spaniards when they arrived in New Spain? (01)
3. How is Cortés portrayed in one of Orozco's frescos? (02)
4. Describe the body of Cortés in that fresco. (02)
5. Who is pictured with Cortés in the same fresco? (03)
6. Describe how Orozco portrays Christian charity. (04)
7. What does Orozco critique? (05)
8. What did many Spanish priests do in New Spain? (06)
9. What do the letters ABCD signify in that fresco? (06)
10. Who built hundreds of convents in New Spain? (06)
11. What does the knotted cord signify? (06)
12. What does the wheel symbolize in another of Orozco's frescos? (07)
13. According to Orozco, how does the wheel change the world? (08)
14. What contrast does Orozco show in that fresco? (09)
15. Describe how Orozco portrays the demagogues. (10)
16. Describe how Orozco portrays the despots. (11)
17. Describe the statue of Bishop Juan Cruz de Cabañas. (12)
18. According to many critics, what is the high point of Orozco's art? (13)
19. Describe that fresco. (13)
20. Mention the possible interpretations of that fresco. (14)

21. What may the main figure in that fresco represent to other critics? (15)

« - » - « - » - « - »

FINAL EXAM

Choose the best answer and indicate it with the appropriate letter.

1. José Clemente Orozco was born in the State of
   (a) Nayarit
   (b)Mazatlán
   (c) Jalisco
   (d) Oaxaca

2. When still young, Orozco's family moved to
   (a) Mexico City
   (b) Guadalajara
   (c) Monterrey
   (d) Oaxaca

3. The young José (Orozco) was impressed with the work of a cartoonist and engraver named
   (a) Diego Rivera
   (b) Dr. Atl
   (c) David Alfaro Siqueiros
   (d) José Guadalupe Posada

4. After the death of his father, José began to study
   (a) agriculture
   (b) art
   (c) law
   (d) medicine

5. During an accident with fireworks, the doctors found it necessary to amputate José's
   (a) leg
   (b) arm
   (c) hand
   (d) foot

6. One of José's first works as a cartoonist is tilted *The House of*
   (a) *Joy*
   (b) *Fear*
   (c) *Terror*
   (d) *Tears*

7. Some critics have compared José's art at this time to that of
   (a) Toulouse-Lautrec
   (b) El Greco
   (c) Rembrandt
   (d) Pablo Picasso

8. In the year 1922, a new Director of Public Education took office. His name was
   (a) José Vasconcelos
   (b) Diego Rivera
   (c) David Alfaro Siqueiros
   (d) José Guadalupe Posada

9. The new Director of Public Education wanted to educate the masses by means of
   (a) free tours of the Palace of Fine Arts
   (b) visits to art museums
   (c) art painted on walls of public buildings
   (d) free art classes

10. One of Orozco's murals is titled Cortés and
   (a) Philip II
   (b) Malinche
   (c) Pizarro
   (d) Xicoténcatl

11. Orozco's mural titled *Banquet of the Rich* shows the wealth of the rich and
   (a) the discontent of the lower class
   (b) their beautiful homes

(c) the improvements made by the Mexican Revolution
(d) new Mexico City of that time

12. One of the symbols of communism is the
(a) hammer
(b) ax
(c) plow
(d) sword

13. In the year 1928, Orozco received a commission from Pomona College to paint a mural called
(a) *Poseidon*
(b) *Apollo*
(c) *Prometheus*
(d) *Zeus*

14. Pandora's box contained
(a) riches
(b) evils
(c) ashes
(d) death

15. Orozco later painted a series of murals titled *Epic of American Civilization* at
(a) Knox College
(b) William & Mary College
(c) Bowdoin College
(d) Dartmouth College

16. In one of the murals in the above series, Orozco paints a mythical white god called
(a) Tlaloc
(b) Quetzalcóatl
(c) Huitzilopochtli
(d) Tonatiuh

17. In the same painting, Cortés is seen standing behind a black cross that represents the death of
(a) the white man
(b) Spain
(c) the indigenous civilization of Mexico
(d) Quetzalcóatl

18. After finishing his murals in the United States, Orozco accepts an invitation to paint murals in the city of
(a) Guadalajara
(b) Monterrey
(c) Oaxaca
(d) Puebla

19. In these murals, one of the major themes is the Mexican Revolution, which took place between 1910 and
(a) 1915
(b) 1920
(c) 1925
(d) 1930

20. In ancient Rome, seekers for public office wore togas of what color?
(a) white
(b) black
(c) red
(d) blue

21. The capital of the State of Jalisco is
(a) Monterrey
(b) Oaxaca
(c) Puebla
(d) Guadalajara

22. The leader who signed the decree abolishing slavery in Mexico was
(a) Miguel Hidalgo

(b) Porfirio Díaz
(c) Pancho Villa
(d) Emiliano Zapata

23. The Cabañas Cultural Institute was originally a(n)
(a) church
(b) orphanage
(c) prison
(d) convent

24. On the ceiling of the Cabañas Cultural Institute, Orozco paints
(a) a horse with two heads
(b) two French painters
(c) King Charles I
(d) the "pentaphasic" man

25. Many critics say that the high point of Orozco's art is his fresco called
(a) Man at the Wheel
(b) Man in Flames
(c) Man at the Crossroads
(d) Man at War

« - » - « - » - « - »

ABOUT THE AUTHOR

Dr. Harry E. Babbitt is a U.S. citizen who for 42 years was a Spanish instructor at high schools and universities. At the same time, he has been and is a meticulous researcher of the Hispano-American culture, which led him to make dozens of trips throughout Spain and Latin America in order to broaden his investigations and supplement them with films, videos and photos. As a result of this extensive experience, he is now publishing bilingual guides at the intermediate level, so students can practice their target language and at the same time learn about the extensive and diverse culture of Spain and Latin America.

ALSO AVAILABLE AT AMAZON

SPANISH & LATIN AMERICAN STUDIES

(THE DIFFICULT MADE EASY)

Recommended for High School and College students' first introduction to cultural and literary masterpieces.

TITLES AVAILABLE
BILINGUAL EDITION

"Paperback" & "Kindle eBooks"
(Search in books: "Harry E. Babbitt Ph. D.")
including those below:

SPANISH HISTORY

History of Moors and Christians in Spain
The Old Road to Santiago in Spain
The Road to Santiago in France
The Road to Santiago in Spain
The Battle of Navas de Tolosa
The Battle of Covadonga
The Battle of Guadalete
Pre-Roman Spain
Visigothic Spain
Islamic Spain
Roman Spain

SPANISH LITERATURE

Don Quijote of La Mancha P 1 Commented and Summarized
Tell me what you read and I'll tell you who you are Annotated
The life of Lazarillo de Tormes and his fortunes and adversities
Gustavo Adolfo Bécquer Rhymes and Legends
Lament for Ignacio Sánchez Mejías Annotated
The Prodigious Shoemaker's Wife Annotated

Sor Juana Inés de la Cruz: The Tenth Muse.
The House of Bernarda Alba Annotated
La Celestina Annotated and Shortened
Brief History of the Spanish Language
Poem of Fernán González Annotated
The Land of Alvargonzález Annotated
San Manuel Bueno, Mártir Annotated
Antonio Machado: Poet of Soria
The Song of My Cid Annotated
Don Juan Tenorio Annotated
Fuente Ovejuna Annotated
Mariana Pineda Annotated
Blood Wedding Annotated
Gypsy Ballads Annotated
Old Spanish Ballads
Yerma Annotated

SPANISH ART

Salvador Dalí and the Hallucinogenic Toreador:
Art and History of Tauromachy
(Bullfighting)
Diego Velázquez and his Spain
Francisco Goya and his Spain
Pablo Picasso and His Spain
Romanesque Art in Spain
El Greco and his Spain
Picasso's Guernica

AMERICA: DISCOVERY & CONQUEST

Friar Bernardino de Sahagún Missionary and Historian
Vasco Núñez de Balboa Discovers the Pacific Ocean
Christopher Columbus Admiral of the Ocean Sea
The True History of the Conquest of New Spain
Ferdinand Magellan Discoverer Extraordinaire
Francisco Pizarro and the Conquest of Peru
Hernán Cortés and the Conquest of México

LATIN AMERICAN HISTORY

Bartolomé de las Casas Protector of the Indians
Inca Garcilaso de la Vega: Royal Commentaries
Miguel Hidalgo and Mexican Independence
José de San Martín Argentine Liberator
Simón Bolívar Venezuelan Liberator
Six Ancient Cultures of Mexico
José Martí Cuban Patriot

LATIN AMERICAN LITERATURE

The Return of Martín Fierro Excerpts Annotated
Domingo Faustino Sarmiento and his Facundo
La Araucana Excerpts Annotated
Martín Fierro Excerpts Annotated
Gabriela Mistral Poet of Chile
Pablo Neruda in his Words:
Pablo Neruda Poet of Chile
Ruben Dario: Modernism
The Popol Vuh

LATIN AMERICAN ART

The Subway of Buenos Aires: its History and Art
Diego Rivera Murals in the National Palace P1
Diego Rivera Murals in the National Palace P2
Mexican Convents of the Sixteenth Century
David Alfaro Siqueiros Mexican Muralist
The Day of the Dead in Mexico
Spanish Heritage in the USA
Cemeteries of Buenos Aires

FOR COMPLETE LISTINGS OR
MORE INFO CONTACT US AT
quiquesatx@gmail.com

HARRY E BABBITT
JOSÉ CLEMENTE OROZCO MEXICAN MURALIST
JOSÉ CLEMENTE OROZCO MURALISTA MEXICANO

JOSÉ CLEMENTE OROZCO MURALISTA MEXICANO

JOSÉ CLEMENTE OROZCO MEXICAN MURALIST

HISTORIA — LITERATURA — ARTE
HISTORY — LITERATURE — ART

Una Guía Bilingüe de Estudios
A Bilingual Study Guide
(Spanish – English)

Estudios Españoles y
Latino-Americanos
(Tomo 65)

Harry E. Babbitt, Ph.D.

ISBN: 9798399671802

DEDICACIÓN

Dedico este libro a todos mis antiguos colegas y estudiantes con quienes he tenido el placer de trabajar durante muchos años de enseñanza en la escuela secundaria y la universidad. Asimismo, deseo agradecer a mis consultores actuales por el arduo trabajo y la dedicación que han demostrado para que esta nueva serie de guías bilingües sea un éxito.

RECONOCIMIENTOS

Educational Consultant (English) — Nancy Frakes, Ph.D.
Editorial Consultant (Spanish) — Mario Taglione
Technical Consultant — Oswaldo Salas
Graphic Design — Luis Ríos

SUGERENCIAS DE USO

Esta guía bilingüe es para hablantes de inglés y español de todas las edades (especialmente estudiantes) que deseen aprender el idioma del otro. Mientras lee en un idioma, uno puede referirse a la otra versión cuando surgen problemas o preguntas.

La vida y obra artística de José Clemente Orozco, tanto en México como en Estados Unidos, se celebran en ambos países. Junto con Diego Rivera y David Alfaro Siqueiros, Orozco es uno de los tres grandes muralistas mexicanos del siglo XX. En este libro, contamos la historia de Orozco para apreciar su importancia en la historia del arte y la política de México durante un momento difícil en la historia mexicana.

Es importante entender y recordar algunas de las personas, lugares y cosas a las que se refieren los capítulos de ***JOSÉ CLEMENTE OROZCO, MURALISTA MEXICANO.*** ¿Por qué no disfrutar aprendiendo inglés o español mientras lees y hablas sobre uno de los muralistas más importantes de los tiempos modernos?

CAPÍTULO UNO
HIJO DE LA REVOLUCIÓN

(01-01) José Clemente Orozco (abajo) quien en el futuro será uno de los "tres grandes" muralistas de México[8], nació en 1883 en el Estado de Jalisco, ubicado al suroeste de México. Para escapar de una vida de pobreza y adversidad, su familia se mudó a la Ciudad de México cuando José era muy joven.

(01-02) Siendo un niño sumamente sensible, fue muy consciente de las penurias de aquella época durante los últimos años de la dictadura de Porfirio Díaz. Aunque el dictador embelleció la capital con nuevos edificios y hermosas avenidas al estilo francés, los pobres seguían sufriendo como en el pasado. Sin duda, José sabía que tarde o temprano iba a estallar un enfrentamiento entre ricos y pobres.

(01-03) Se cuenta que un día, cuando José iba caminando a clase, vio al dibujante y grabador José Guadalupe Posada trabajando junto al escaparate de su

[8] Los otros dos grandes muralistas mexicanos del siglo XX fueron Diego Rivera y David Alfaro Siqueiros.

imprenta que daba a la calle (abajo). En el futuro, este gran artista se hará famoso por sus viñetas y dibujos satíricos sobre la vida mexicana a principios del siglo XX. Por este medio informaba al público sobre los diferentes acontecimientos del día con sus originales y divertidas caricaturas.

(01-04) Aunque los divertidos dibujos de Posada (como "La Calavera Catrina", abajo) podrían haber despertado en la mente del joven José su primera noción de que el arte podía ser un medio poderoso para protestar contra ciertos aspectos de la vida mexicana, en ese momento estaba preocupado por otros problemas más apremiantes.

(01-05) Los padres de José decidieron que su hijo debería empezar a pensar en elegir una profesión, porque ya tenía quince años. Así, lo enviaron a una escuela para que comenzara sus estudios de ingeniero agrónomo. Por supuesto, José no tenía ningún interés en tal carrera. A los pocos meses José contrajo fiebre reumática y regresó a casa para recuperarse. Al mismo tiempo, su padre sufría de tifus y murió poco después, dejando a José a cargo del cuidado de su madre.

(01-06) El único resultado bueno de estas dificultades fue que ahora se sentía libre para dedicar su vida al estudio del arte, su verdadera pasión. Sin perder tiempo, comenzó a tomar clases de arte en la famosa Academia de San Carlos (abajo). Para mantener a su madre y pagar sus gastos personales, obtuvo pequeños trabajos como dibujante o diseñador en una empresa de arquitectura.

(01-07) Ahora todo parecía bien en su vida, pero muy pronto le sobrevino otra tragedia. Se acercaba el 16 de septiembre de 1904, Día de la Independencia de México (abajo). José decidió fabricar sus propios fuegos artificiales para celebrar ese día tan especial. Mientras mezclaba los productos químicos se produjo una explosión. Aunque sufrió graves quemaduras, no consultó a tiempo a un médico y pronto tuvieron que amputarle la mano izquierda. Sin embargo, a pesar de tantos percances, José pudo continuar con su carrera artística. En el año 1909 decide dedicar todos sus esfuerzos a la pintura.

(01-08) La Revolución Mexicana ya había comenzado y el país estaba a punto de sufrir una década de luchas políticas y sociales en la que morirían miles de personas. Entre 1911 y 1916, José trabajó como dibujante en varias editoriales donde produjo una serie de acuarelas titulada *La casa de las lágrimas*, que retrataba la vida a menudo sórdida de los barrios populares de la Ciudad de México (siguiente página, primera foto).

(01-09) Algunos críticos de arte han comparado las obras de Orozco de este período con las del artista francés Toulouse-Lautrec, famoso por sus pinturas de la vida parisina en cafés, cabarets y casas de mala reputación (siguiente página segunda foto). En la obra de ambos artistas se nota la compasión que ambos tenían por los problemas de la "gente de la calle". Al mismo tiempo, José optó por criticar la sociedad mexicana de aquellos años difíciles de principios del siglo XX.

« - » - « - » - « - »

NOTA BIOGRÁFICA
JOSÉ GUADALUPE POSADA

José Guadalupe Posada fue un extraordinario dibujante y grabador que nació en Aguascalientes en el año 1852. Luego de pasar un tiempo en León, Guanajuato, se mudó a la Ciudad de México en 1887, donde abrió su propia imprenta. Allí comenzó a ilustrar romances populares que trataban sobre acontecimientos políticos, crímenes terribles e incluso predicciones del fin del mundo. Hoy Posada es famoso por sus innumerables "Calaveras" (obituarios de personas vivas) y esqueletos que utilizó para criticar los males de la sociedad mexicana durante la dictadura de Porfirio Díaz. Esta era su manera de criticar a los ricos y poderosos de manera humorística. Posada murió pobre en el año 1913 después del comienzo de la Revolución Mexicana.

« - » - « - » - « - »

ACTIVIDADES

1. Lee más sobre José Clemente Orozco.
   https://es.wikipedia.org/wiki/Jos%C3%A9_Clemente_Orozco
2. Lee acerca de Porfirio Díaz.
   https://es.wikipedia.org/wiki/Porfirio_D%C3%ADaz
3. Lee sobre "La Calavera Catrina".
   https://es.wikipedia.org/wiki/La_Catrina
4. Lee acerca de la Academia de San Carlos.
   https://es.wikipedia.org/wiki/Academia_de_San_Carlos
5. Lee sobre la Revolución Mexicana.
   https://es.wikipedia.org/wiki/Revoluci%C3%B3n_mexicana
6. Lee acerca de Toulouse-Lautrec.
   https://es.wikipedia.org/wiki/Henri_de_Toulouse-Lautrec

CAPÍTULO UNO: PREGUNTAS

1. ¿Quiénes fueron los tres grandes muralistas mexicanos? (01) (Nota # 1)
2. ¿Dónde nació (José) Orozco? ¿En qué año? (01)
3. ¿Por qué se mudó la familia de José a la Ciudad de México? (01)
4. ¿Quién era el dictador de México en ese momento? (02)
5. ¿Cómo embelleció Porfirio Díaz la Ciudad de México? (02)
6. ¿Quién fue José Guadalupe Posada? (03)
7. ¿Qué representaba la "Calavera Catrina"? (04)
8. ¿Qué querían los padres de José que estudiara su hijo? (05)
9. ¿Por qué José volvió a casa? (05)
10. Explica lo que le pasó al padre de José. (05)
11. ¿Adónde fue José a estudiar arte? (06)
12. ¿Cómo apoyó José a su madre? (06)
13. Explica qué le pasó a José el día de la Independencia de México de 1904. (07)
14. ¿Qué hizo José entre 1911 y 1916? (08)
15. ¿Qué retrató la serie de acuarelas de José *La casa de las lágrimas*? (08)
16. ¿Quién fue Toulouse-Lautrec? (09)
17. Explica cómo era el estilo de arte de José a principios del siglo XX. (09)

« - » - « - » - « - »

CAPITULO DOS
OROZCO Y EL MOVIMIENTO MURALISTA

(02-01) Un hito importante en la vida artística de José Clemente Orozco ocurre en el año 1922, cuando se une a Diego Rivera y David Alfaro Siqueiros para iniciar un movimiento muralista en México. Durante la presidencia de Álvaro Obregón (1920-24), José Vasconcelos (abajo) fue nombrado Secretario de Educación Pública. Reorganizó la biblioteca nacional y creó varios departamentos de Bellas Artes y dirigió un programa para publicar obras de autores clásicos en ediciones asequibles para el público. Vasconcelos también trajo a México a eminentes educadores y artistas[9] en un intento por mejorar la instrucción después de tantos años de guerra. Uno de sus proyectos más importantes cambió la historia del arte en México.

[9] Entre estos artistas estaban Diego Rivera, Jean Charlot, Fernando Leal, David Alfaro Siqueiros, Ramón Alva de la Canal, Fermín Revueltas. Posteriormente, José Clemente Orozco participó en el proyecto.

(02-02) Vasconcelos convenció a varios destacados pintores para que colaboraran con él en su empeño de educar a las masas por medio de murales pintados en los muros de edificios públicos como el "Antiguo Colegio de San Ildefonso". Este edificio en el centro histórico de la Ciudad de México había sido la residencia de los estudiantes jesuitas y luego se convirtió en la Escuela Nacional Preparatoria. Finalmente, en el año 1992, se convirtió en uno de los museos más importantes de la capital mexicana (abajo).

(02-03) Fue aquí donde varios artistas pintaron murales con temas mexicanos, especialmente la Revolución. Así, poco a poco, surgió un movimiento nacionalista, didáctico y popular para poner en práctica el concepto de “arte callejero” con una ideología claramente izquierdista. José Clemente Orozco participó de este movimiento encabezado por Vasconcelos al pintar unos frescos en los muros norte de los tres niveles del patio principal, teniendo como tema la Revolución Mexicana.

(02-04) Los primeros murales de Orozco se pueden ver en el Antiguo Colegio de San Ildefonso donde el joven

José había estudiado años antes. Una copia del fresco que se ve abajo se llama *Maternidad* y es la única imagen de una obra que queda de la parte original del proyecto en dicho Colegio (abajo). Algunos dicen que muestra la gran influencia del arte renacentista europeo, quizás de Botticelli.

(02-05) En ese momento muchas personas criticaron la obra porque había pintado una Virgen desnuda con el Niño. Sin embargo, Orozco declaró que no era su intención pintar una virgen, sino solo una madre (siguiente página primera foto). Finalmente, el mismo Orozco decidió destruir la obra para tener un cuarto donde pintar uno de sus murales que hoy vemos en el mismo lugar.

(02-06) Otro de los murales de Orozco en el Antiguo Colegio de San Ildefonso es una obra titulada *Hernán Cortés y la Malinche* (siguiente página segunda foto). Era una joven india que se convirtió en la amante del conquistador. A sus pies yace el hijo pequeño que tuvieron juntos. (Ver Nota de Historia) Las tres figuras están desnudas, algo similar a Adán y Eva. Algunos dicen que su descendencia tal vez represente una nación maltratada y degenerada por la mezcla de razas. Se puede notar el contraste entre la blancura de Cortés y el tradicional color indio oscuro de la Malinche. No está claro si Cortés está mostrando un gesto protector o dominante hacia la Malinche. Sin embargo, es evidente que Orozco la pinta como la madre de México, pero no sabemos si cree que eso es bueno o malo.

(02-07) También en el Antiguo Colegio de San Ildefonso, Orozco pintó algunas escenas quizás explicativas de algunas de las causas de la Revolución Mexicana, una de las cuales fue la brecha entre ricos y pobres. El mural de abajo titulado *Banquete de los Ricos* muestra el gran descontento de la clase baja en ese momento.

(02-08) En la parte superior del mural vemos el banquete de los ricos, bien vestidos, disfrutando de una buena comida y divirtiéndose a costa de los pobres (siguiente página primera foto). Orozco usa colores brillantes para señalar objetos y personas importantes. El fondo naranja sugiere un fuego y enfatiza la intensidad del ambiente o las relaciones entre las masas ricas y las empobrecidas. El tono en general refleja la interacción hostil entre los dos grupos.

(02-09) En la parte inferior de la misma obra, vemos a tres hombres con sus herramientas cotidianas que representan a la clase obrera en su lucha diaria por sobrevivir en un país gobernado por la élite. El dedo de un hombre rico señala el martillo, que es uno de los símbolos del comunismo (página siguiente, segunda foto). Recordemos que la

Revolución Rusa comenzó en 1917 al mismo tiempo que los pobres de México luchaban contra un gobierno que los explotaba.

« « - » - « - » - « - »

NOTA DE HISTORIA #1
MALINCHE — DOÑA MARINA

La Malinche (siguiente página), también conocida con el nombre de Doña Marina, fue una de las veinte esclavas entregadas como tributo a Hernán Cortés cuando derrotó a los guerreros indios en la región de Tabasco en el año 1519.

Malinche hablaba la lengua de los aztecas y también la de los mayas. Aprendió castellano y sirvió a los españoles como intérprete durante la conquista de México. Además, Doña Marina informó a los españoles sobre las costumbres sociales y militares de los indígenas de México. Uno de los conquistadores dijo una vez que "después de Dios, la razón principal del éxito de la conquista de México fue Doña Marina". Hoy todos saben que doña Marina se convirtió en la amante de Cortés. Después de la conquista de Tenochtitlán en 1521, dio a luz un hijo con Cortés llamado Martín, quien sería uno de los primeros "mestizos" (personas de sangre mixta) nacidos en México.

Hoy en México la palabra "malinchismo" se refiere a personas que prefieren un estilo de vida diferente a su propia cultura o una vida con influencias extranjeras. Algunos mexicanos creen que la Malinche traicionó a los indígenas al apoyar a los españoles en la conquista de México. Por otro lado, algunos la ven como la figura fundadora de la nación mexicana. En los últimos años, Doña Marina se ha convertido en una figura mitad mítica y mitad legendaria. Su vida ha sido el tema de muchas películas y obras literarias.

« - » - « - » - « - »

NOTA DE HISTORIA #2
EL CORRIDO MEXICANO

El corrido mexicano es una narración popular en forma de canción, poesía o balada (abajo). Antes de la popularidad de la radio y la televisión y los medios electrónicos, el corrido se utilizaba para informar y educar al público, especialmente a la clase baja, sobre los acontecimientos que ocurrían en el país como la Revolución Mexicana. Muchos corridos celebraron las hazañas de héroes como Pancho Villa y Emiliano Zapata. La popularidad de los corridos se debió a su lenguaje sencillo y música agradable. Algunos de los corridos favoritos de esa época eran La Cucaracha, Adelita y La Valentina.

En la actualidad, los corridos han tenido un gran desarrollo y están dedicados al recuerdo de hechos importantes y personajes ilustres de un período que ya ha pasado a la historia. A continuación, citamos el corrido de Gabino Palomares (siguiente página) llamado *La Maldición de la Malinche*, que se puede escuchar en YouTube.

« - » - « - » - « - »

NOTA DE HISTORIA #3
LA CUCARACHA

Sin duda el corrido más famoso de la Revolución Mexicana es "La Cucaracha". La canción es reconocida en casi todo el mundo. Se trata de una cucaracha que ha perdido una de sus seis patas e intenta caminar con las cinco que le quedan. La letra y el ritmo de la canción imitan el paso irregular que usa la cucaracha para caminar.

Se dice que los soldados mexicanos cantaban corridos como este durante sus largas marchas por los desiertos y montañas de México. Hay decenas de versiones diferentes de las palabras que varían según los caprichos políticos del momento y el lugar. Algunos dicen que la letra se refiere a Pancho Villa porque sus largos brazos y piernas sobresalen del Ford Modelo-T que usaba. En otra ocasión hace alusiones a Victoriano Huerta porque se dice que fumaba marihuana En cualquier caso, la canción se burla y ridiculiza a todos.

« - » - « - » - « - »

ACTIVIDADES

1. Lee sobre Diego Rivera. https://es.wikipedia.org/wiki/Diego_Rivera
2. Lee acerca de David Alfaro Siqueiros. https://es.wikipedia.org/wiki/David_Alfaro_Siqueiros
3. Lee sobre José Vasconcelos. https://es.wikipedia.org/wiki/Jos%C3%A9_Vasconcelos
4. Lee acerca del Colegio de San Ildefonso. https://es.wikipedia.org/wiki/Antiguo_Colegio_de_San_Ildefonso
5. Lee sobre el Corrido mexicano. https://es.wikipedia.org/wiki/Corrido_(M%C3%A9xico)
6. Escuche el corrido llamado *La Maldición de la Malinche.* https://www.youtube.com/watch?v=vEVQiw7ROog
7. Escuche el corrido llamado *Adelita*. https://www.youtube.com/watch?v=EoR1dyGhGt8

« - » - « - » - « - »

CAPÍTULO DOS: PREGUNTAS

1. ¿Qué hito logró José en el año 1922? (01)
2. ¿Quién fue José Vasconcelos? Describa sus logros. (01)
3. ¿Quién colaboró con José Vasconcelos? ¿Con qué propósito? (02)
4. ¿Qué ocurrió en el año 1922? (02)
5. ¿Cuál fue el tema del llamado “arte callejero”? (03)
6. Describe el fresco de Orozco llamado *Maternidad*. (04)
7. ¿Por qué critican algunos críticos el cuadro *Maternidad*? (05)
8. ¿Quién fue la Malinche? (06) (Nota de Historia # 1).

9. Describe lo que dicen algunos sobre el cuadro Hernán Cortés y la Malinche. (06)
10. ¿Cuál es el título de uno de los murales de Orozco sobre la Revolución Mexicana? (07)
11. Describe el mural de Orozco titulado *Banquete de los ricos*. (08)
12. ¿Qué representa el martillo? (09)
13. ¿En qué año comenzó la Revolución Rusa? (09)

« - » - « - » - « - »

CAPÍTULO TRES
MURAL DE OROZCO EN POMONA COLLEGE

(03-01) En el año 1928, Orozco inicia el segundo capítulo de su vida artística con un viaje a los Estados Unidos. Allí abrió una exposición de sus *Dibujos de la Revolución* que tuvo un éxito notable y así José pudo cubrir el costo de sus necesidades básicas. Poco tiempo después, recibió el encargo de pintar un mural en Pomona College en Claremont, California. Fue aquí, en el comedor de Frary Hall, donde Orozco fue el primero de los "tres grandes" pintores mexicanos en pintar un mural en Estados Unidos. José llegó a Claremont en marzo de 1930 y trabajó durante tres meses pintando un mural llamado Prometheus que se puede ver al fondo del comedor (abajo).

(03-02) Antes de comentar la trascendencia de esta obra de Orozco, conviene hablar brevemente de Prometeo. Al repasar un poco de esta interesante historia, podemos comprender mejor el importante mensaje de este mural.

(03-03) *En la mitología griega, Prometeo era uno de los Titanes (un grupo de deidades poderosas), descendientes* *de Gaia (La Tierra) y Urano (Cielo) que gobernaron durante la Edad de Oro de Grecia. Uno de los mitos griegos cuenta cómo Prometeo engañó a Zeus (dios del cielo y rey de los dioses del monte Olimpo). Se cuenta que Prometeo preparó un sacrificio a Zeus y lo dividió en dos partes. Una parte contenía las entrañas y la carne. En la otra parte, Prometeo colocó los huesos cubiertos con una sabrosa salsa, luego le pidió a Zeus que eligiera la parte que él prefería, Zeus eligió la parte que tenía la salsa pensando que sería más apetecible.*

(03-04) *Cuando Zeus calentó la parte que había elegido, descubrió que no eran más que huesos. Zeus se enfureció y le quitó el fuego al Hombre. En poco tiempo, Prometeo ascendió al Monte Olimpo y robó fuego del carro de Helios quien, según otro mito, llevaba el sol por el cielo todos los días en dicho carro. Zeus vuelve a mostrar su furia cuando le ordena a Hefesto (dios del sol y de la fragua) que cree una mujer de arcilla que se llamará Pandora. Algún tiempo después, Zeus envió a Pandora a la casa del hermano de Prometeo. Este último tenía en su casa una caja cerrada donde guardaba todos los males del mundo, como las peores plagas y enfermedades* (siguiente página primera foto). *Cuando Pandora llegó a la casa del hermano, encontró la caja y la abrió, exponiendo así a la humanidad a todas estas abominaciones. ¿Quién no ha oído hablar de la famosa caja de Pandora?*

(03-05) Para los griegos, Prometeo era importante porque creía que le había dado el don del fuego al Hombre para que todos se beneficiaran de la luz y del progreso en forma de las artes, las ciencias y la civilización en general.

(03-06) Orozco pintó la gigantesca figura de Prometeo que domina todo el mural. Las llamas rojas iluminan el cuerpo del Titán. En el momento de arrebatarle el sol para traerlo a la Tierra, sus manos parecen fundirse en las llamas como en un cuadro cubista abstracto. A ambos lados de Prometeo, hay grupos de mortales terrenales, retorciéndose en diferentes estados de tormento y angustia (abajo, derecha).

(03-07) El detalle en la siguiente página representa el momento en que Prometeo entrega el fuego a los seres humanos. La humanidad ha sufrido la opresión, y ahora, con el regalo del Titán ante ellos, las reacciones son diversas. Algunos parecen estar aterrorizados, mientras que otros demuestran su entusiasmo.

(03-08) Quizás la lección para los seres humanos, hoy como en los siglos pasados, sea saber aprovechar al máximo los dones que hemos recibido. Estos vienen en forma de inteligencia que podemos usar para salir de la oscuridad y mejorar nuestras vidas. Al mismo tiempo, la Humanidad debe tener cuidado porque la misma llama que purifica también puede quemar y destruir todo lo que toca. La moraleja de este mural le confiere un atractivo universal para todos los tiempos.

« - » - « - » - « - »

ACTIVIDADES

1. Lee más sobre Prometeo.
   https://es.wikipedia.org/wiki/Prometeo
2. Lee más acerca de la Caja de Pandora.
   https://es.wikipedia.org/wiki/Caja_de_Pandora

« - » - « - » - « - »

CAPÍTULO TRES: PREGUNTAS

1. ¿En qué año llegó Orozco a los Estados Unidos? (01)
2. ¿Cómo se llamó la exposición inaugural de Orozco? (01)
3. ¿De dónde recibió Orozco el encargo de pintar un mural? (01)
4. ¿Cómo se llamó el primer mural de Orozco? (01)
5. ¿Cuánto tiempo le tomó a Orozco pintar su primer mural? (01)
6. ¿Quién fue Prometeo? (03)
7. Describe el sacrificio que Prometeo preparó a Zeus. (03)
8. ¿Qué parte eligió Zeus y cuál fue el resultado? (03) (04)
9. ¿Qué robó Prometeo del carro de Helios? (04)
10. ¿Cómo mostró Zeus su furia nuevamente? (04)
11. ¿Quién fue Pandora? (04)
12. ¿Qué encerró en una caja el hermano de Prometeo? (04)
13. ¿Por qué fue importante Prometeo para los griegos? (05)
14. Describe el mural de Prometeo de Orozco. (06)
15. Describe el momento en que Prometeo entrega el fuego a los seres humanos. (07)
16. ¿Cuál es la moraleja del mural de Orozco para la Humanidad? (08)

« - » - « - » - « - »

CAPÍTULO CUATRO
MURALES DE OROZCO EN DARTMOUTH COLLEGE

(04-01) Entre 1932 y 1934, Orozco pintó una serie de murales llamada *La Epopeya de la Civilización Americana* en la Biblioteca Baker del Dartmouth College en Hanover, New Hampshire. Como tema eligió el impacto que tuvo en el continente norteamericano el choque de diferentes culturas, tanto nativas como europeas. Como punto de partida en el estudio de este tema, debemos tener en cuenta que Dartmouth College (abajo) se fundó en el año 1769 para brindar instrucción a los nativos americanos. En sus clases los maestros blancos enseñaban las ideas básicas sobre la Cultura Occidental. De esta manera intentaron eliminar el uso de las lenguas y creencias indígenas. Con el paso de los siglos, Dartmouth College se convirtió en una de las instituciones de educación superior más prestigiosas de los Estados Unidos, pero los indios casi han desaparecido.

(04-02) Orozco trabajó casi dos años para completar una serie de veinticuatro murales que cubren diferentes aspectos de la interesante historia de algunas de las civilizaciones indígenas de América del Norte y cómo influyeron en la vida de los colonos y eventos futuros en el desarrollo de la civilización "americana" de hoy. Vamos a analizar brevemente algunos de los paneles más significativos (abajo). Los diez primeros tratan de la migración de los indios a América del Norte. Al principio, los nativos recién llegados estaban solos y muchos estaban asustados. Así, crearon dioses y les ofrecieron sacrificios humanos a cambio de su protección y benevolencia.

(04-03) En otro panel (siguiente página) vemos un lugar dividido entre el mundo espiritual y el físico. Quetzalcóatl[10], el mítico dios blanco de los toltecas, ha llegado y está desenterrando a los antiguos dioses que portan curiosas máscaras. Es el "Dios Civilizador" y "Maestro de los Hombres" que, según la tradición, está iniciando una nueva época en la que enseña a los pueblos originarios los elementos básicos de la agricultura y las artes. Como resultado de sus enseñanzas, el pueblo ha construido magníficas pirámides y la civilización continúa progresando durante muchos siglos hasta llegar a una Edad de Oro para los pueblos indígenas de esa época.

---

[10] Quetzalcóatl — La "Serpiente Emplumada".

(04-04) Una de las muchas leyendas nos dice que Quetzalcóatl se opone a los sacrificios humanos tan populares entre los dioses más antiguos. Para vengarse, los enemigos de Quetzalcóatl le gastan una broma y se emborracha y hace que una mujer pierda su honor. Avergonzado de tal acto y convencido de que no puede hacer más por su pueblo, Quetzalcóatl se dirige a la costa del Golfo de México. Allí se convierte en el "Lucero del Alba" y se despide de sus súbditos. Antes de partir, promete volver con su pueblo en una fecha determinada que coincide con la llegada de los españoles en el año 1519. Al ver a Cortés, muchos nativos creen naturalmente que Quetzalcóatl, su bendito dios blanco, ha regresado.

(04-05) En la siguiente página vemos a Cortés de pie junto a la cruz. El color predominante es el negro que simboliza la muerte de la hermosa civilización indígena de México. Se reemplaza por las máquinas que se ven en el lado derecho del mural. Para Orozco, estos representan el comienzo de la "Era de la Tecnología" que muchos disfrutan hoy.

(04-06) A medida que pasamos a otro panel, notamos las diversas diferencias entre la América anglosajona a la izquierda (siguiente página primera foto) y la América hispana a la derecha. El personaje principal en la América anglosajona[11] es la maestra con su Biblia. Sus compatriotas parecen estar disfrutando de la paz, el dinero y el orden. Para Orozco todos están cortados del mismo molde. Los niños y los ancianos visten iguales en varios tonos de gris. Por otro lado, el personaje principal de Hispanoamérica es un humilde soldado de la Revolución Mexicana. Está rodeado de políticos y generales corruptos que han traído la guerra, la destrucción, la pobreza, la miseria y la muerte a la patria.

(04-07) En el mural titulado *Dioses del Mundo Moderno*, Orozco criticó duramente el sistema educativo en los Estados Unidos (siguiente página segunda foto). Al fondo vemos a varios profesores que adoptan la forma de esqueletos o momias ataviados con sus tradicionales túnicas

---

[11] Anglosajón — los anglosajones eran inmigrantes del norte de Europa que se establecieron en Inglaterra en los siglos quinto y sexto. Compuestos inicialmente por muchos grupos pequeños y divididos en varios reinos, los anglosajones finalmente se unieron en un solo reino político: el reino de Inglaterra.

y gorros. Más abajo notamos un esqueleto femenino (muestra la influencia del caricaturista José Guadalupe Posada) que está pariendo un embrión muerto similar a los otros que vemos en sus pequeños ataúdes de vidrio. Para Orozco, estos fetos sin vida son símbolos del conocimiento inútil contenido en los libros oscuros, casi negros, al lado de la madre.

(04-08) Muchos críticos de arte han señalado que es irónico que Orozco fuera invitado a pintar un mural en la biblioteca del Dartmouth College que fue fundado precisamente para convertir a los indígenas a la religión y costumbres de los anglosajones de Nueva Inglaterra. Hoy Dartmouth College es un centro de tecnología y aprendizaje que representa todos los "males" que Orozco pintó en sus murales por los que pasan diariamente los estudiantes camino a sus clases.

(04-09) Los paneles restantes de los frescos de Orozco en Dartmouth aluden a la civilización moderna como una amenaza para la supervivencia de las razas indígenas de América del Norte. En Estados Unidos queda poco de esa antigua cultura, especialmente en Nueva Inglaterra[12]. Por otra parte, en México aún viven varios millones de indios y continúan hablando más de cincuenta lenguas nativas. Aunque algunos ahora se comunican por celular y ven telenovelas en la televisión, han podido conservar muchas de sus costumbres del pasado (abajo).

---

12 Nueva Inglaterra: territorio al noreste de los Estados Unidos que incluye seis estados: Maine, New Hampshire, Vermont, Massachusetts, Connecticut y Rhode Island.

ACTIVIDADES

1. Lee acerca de Quetzalcóatl.
https://es.wikipedia.org/wiki/Quetzalc%C3%B3atl

« - » - « - » - « - »

CAPÍTULO CUATRO: PREGUNTAS

1. ¿Dónde pintó Orozco su segunda serie de frescos en los Estados Unidos? (01)
2. ¿Qué tema eligió Orozco para esta serie de frescos? (01)
3. ¿En qué año se fundó Dartmouth College? ¿Con qué propósito? (01)
4. Explica el tema de los diez primeros de la serie de veinticuatro murales. (02)
5. ¿Quién fue Quetzalcóatl? (03)
6. ¿Qué enseñó Quetzalcóatl a su pueblo? (03)
7. ¿Cuál fue la consecuencia de la broma de los enemigos de Quetzalcóatl? (04)
8. Antes de partir, ¿qué prometió hacer Quetzalcóatl? (04)
9. ¿Qué ocurrió en el año 1519? (04)
10. Describe cómo aparece Cortés en el mural. (05)
11. ¿Qué representan las máquinas en este mural? (05)
12. ¿Quiénes eran los anglosajones? (06)
13. Describe cómo retrata Orozco a la América anglosajona en este mural. (06)
14. Describe cómo retrata Orozco a Hispanoamérica en el mismo mural. (06)
15. Describe el mural titulado Dioses del mundo moderno. (07)
16. ¿Qué influencia es evidente en este mural? (07)
17. ¿Qué ironía han señalado algunos críticos? (08)
18. Describa lo que enseña Dartmouth College en la actualidad. (08)

19. ¿A qué se refieren los paneles restantes? (09)
20. Explica en qué se diferencia Estados Unidos de México en la vida de los pueblos indígenas. (09)

« - » - « - » - « - »

CAPÍTULO CINCO
OROZCO EN GUADALAJARA

(05-01) Después de terminar sus bien recibidos murales en las universidades de Pomona y Dartmouth, Orozco regresa a México. Decide aceptar la invitación del gobernador del estado de Jalisco para pintar murales en tres de las instituciones más destacadas de Guadalajara — la Universidad de Guadalajara, el Palacio de Gobierno del Estado de Jalisco y el Hospicio de Cabañas. Orozco dedicará cinco años de su vida a crear lo que se considerará su obra maestra más importante. Abajo vemos la fachada de la universidad que hoy es un museo.

(05-02) Uno de los murales de Orozco en la universidad fue pintado en el Paraninfo del auditorio donde los funcionarios de la universidad realizaban sus reuniones. El mural se llama *El pueblo y sus falsos líderes*. Aquí Orozco critica el monopolio de la educación por parte de la clase rica y privilegiada durante el reinado de la dictadura de Porfirio Díaz, que duró aproximadamente treinta años y finalizó en

1911. Abajo se muestra la interpretación de Diego Rivera de Porfirio Díaz en el centro, su esposa y José Liminatour, su Ministro de Hacienda.

(05-03) El mural de Orozco muestra la gran disparidad entre los ricos, los llamados "hombres de las compañías" o dueños de las grandes haciendas y las masas pobres e incultas (siguiente página primera foto). A la izquierda están los hombres de los dueños de las "haciendas" con sus fusiles y garrotes que gobiernan la vida de las masas que cultivan los campos. El general en la parte superior parece estar observando el enfrentamiento de abajo. Notamos en la parte inferior de este detalle que los ricos son los únicos que tienen libros. Los personajes de la derecha parecen estar dando una conferencia o sermón a los pobres, mientras un hombre los señala con una espada. Esta lucha condujo eventualmente a la Revolución Mexicana que duró aproximadamente diez años (1910-1920).

(05-04) En el lado derecho del mural (siguiente página segunda foto), los trabajadores muestran signos de hambre o incluso de inanición. Las diferentes expresiones faciales muestran la ira y el desprecio que tienen por sus amos. Los opresores parecen apuntar a sus libros para justificar su represión a los trabajadores. Las llamas entre los dos bandos quizás sugieran la revolución sangrienta que está a punto de estallar cuando los autoritarios sean devorados por las llamas.

(05-05) Mientras nos asomamos a la cúpula del auditorio, vemos otro de los hermosos murales de Orozco llamado *El hombre creativo y rebelde* (abajo). Lo primero que notamos es el gran contraste entre los personajes del mural anterior y los de esta cúpula. Vemos que Orozco ha pintado cuatro figuras humanas masculinas, tres de ellas ascendentes. Estos, sin duda, simbolizan la enseñanza, la técnica y la ciencia. Tres de los hombres representados están desnudos y pueden representar la pureza física, moral, intelectual y espiritual. En la parte superior, el ahorcado probablemente esté siendo castigado por su rebelión. En la parte inferior vemos a un hombre pentafásico[13] de dos cabezas que representa la ciencia con sus ramas.

[13] Pentafásico — hombre con múltiples miradas, evoca las infinitas regiones del intelecto.

(05-06) Ahora separemos el mural y miremos a cada uno de los cuatro hombres y consideremos lo que cada uno puede representar. Al mismo tiempo, no debemos olvidar que existen diversas interpretaciones de cada parte de este mural. Comenzamos con un primer plano del llamado hombre "pentafásico", quizás un hombre sabio o un científico (abajo). Cada una de esas cinco cabezas o caras es quizás una manifestación de una sola persona. Aparece desnudo y está rodeado de varios elementos que sugieren una variedad de funciones. En su mano derecha sostiene un escalímetro y en su mano izquierda un compás. Una cara parece estar mirando líneas geométricas y proyecciones dibujadas en blanco. En la punta del compás observamos algunas partes anatómicas como el corazón y el sistema digestivo. La pequeña figura en negro en la parte inferior parece ser un cuerpo con un cráneo trepanado, quizás representando la medicina. Debajo de su mano izquierda hay unas hojas de papel que podrían evocar literatura y leyes.

(05-07) El segundo hombre puede ser jornalero u obrero (siguiente página). Parece agarrar los controles de una poderosa máquina de metal futurista que controla con su mano derecha. Este hombre parece estar orgulloso de su trabajo. Un crítico ha observado que la fusión de su mano con la cabeza del "rebelde" podría sugerir que está esperando el momento adecuado para unirse a él mediante un acto de rebelión.

(05-08) El hombre de la siguiente página podríamos llamarlo el "rebelde". En el mural parece estar cayendo, pero aquí lo hemos puesto boca abajo para que se vea mejor. Este hombre que ha sido ahorcado aparece como un ser místico. Su antebrazo está cubierto con un manto rojo. Dado que la mano del trabajador (como se mencionó anteriormente) parece unirse a la cabeza del rebelde, esta puede ser una forma de transmisión del conocimiento.

(05-09) En contraste con el "rebelde", vemos a un hombre pulcramente vestido de blanco que aquí parece tener un significado especial. En la antigua Roma, los aspirantes a cargos vestían una toga blanca reluciente, presumiblemente para indicar la pureza de sus intenciones cuando buscaban un papel en los asuntos cívicos. El hombre de blanco es el candidato que va a cambiar la condición[14]. En este caso debemos considerar a qué "condición" se refiere Orozco. Lo más probable es que sea el marcado contraste entre ricos y pobres durante la Revolución Mexicana. La función de este hombre de blanco es la de un maestro (siguiente página). Levanta el brazo derecho hacia el "rebelde" y lo señala con el dedo índice. Quizás este maestro pueda ser la inspiración para el cambio en el México del futuro.

[14] Candidato —Observe la interesante etimología de la palabra. Significa "blanco brillante" como las togas que usaban los romanos que buscaban un cargo.

« - » - « - » - « - »

ACTIVIDADES

1. Lee más acerca de la Revolución Mexicana. https://es.wikipedia.org/wiki/Revoluci%C3%B3n_mexicana
2. Lee más sobre el Palacio de Gobierno de Guadalajara. https://es.wikipedia.org/wiki/Palacio_de_Gobierno_de_Jalisco

« - » - « - » - « - »

CAPÍTULO CINCO: PREGUNTAS

1. Después de regresar a México, ¿a dónde fue a pintar Orozco? (01)
2. ¿Cuántos años de su vida dedicó Orozco a pintar sus obras maestras? (01)
3. Describe el mural de Orozco titulado *El pueblo y sus falsos líderes*. (02)
4. ¿Quién fue Porfirio Díaz? (02)

5. ¿Quién fue José Limantour? (02)
6. ¿Qué es una hacienda? (03)
7. Describe a los "hombres de las compañías". (03)
8. ¿Qué causó la Revolución Mexicana? ¿Cuánto duró? (03)
9. Describe el lado derecho del mural. (04)
10. Describe el mural llamado *El hombre creativo y rebelde*. (05)
11. ¿Quién podría ser el "hombre pentafásico"? (06)
12. ¿A quién podrían pertenecer las cinco cabezas o caras? (06)
13. ¿Qué tiene este hombre en su mano derecha? ¿En su mano izquierda? (06)
14. ¿Qué está mirando uno de sus rostros? (06)
15. ¿Qué vemos en la punta de su compás? (06)
16. Describe la figura en negro. (06)
17. ¿Qué vemos debajo de su mano izquierda? (06)
18. Describe al obrero. (07)
19. ¿Qué ha observado un crítico? (07)
20. Describe al "rebelde". (08)
21. ¿Cuál puede ser la forma del "rebelde" de transmitir conocimientos? (08)
22. ¿Qué representa el hombre vestido de blanco? (09)
23. ¿Cuál podría ser la función del hombre vestido de blanco?" (09)
24. ¿Cuál puede ser su relación con el "rebelde"? (09)

« - » - « - » - « - »

CAPÍTULO SEIS
OROZCO EN EL PALACIO DE GOBIERNO

(06-01) En el año 1948, Orozco inicia su última obra monumental en el Palacio de Gobierno en la Plaza de Armas de Guadalajara. Este hermoso edificio data del año 1790. Su estilo barroco, quizás un poco severo, le da a la estructura una sensación de noble austeridad (abajo).

(06-02) Las elegantes columnas y bellos arcos de medio punto del patio interior (siguiente página primera foto) son joyas de la arquitectura civil del siglo XVIII. Alrededor de los amplios corredores se encuentran diferentes salones donde el visitante puede conocer la historia de Guadalajara, capital del Estado de Jalisco.

(06-03) En este edificio el Padre Hidalgo firmó el decreto de abolición de la esclavitud el 6 de diciembre de 1810. En la siguiente página segunda foto, Orozco retrata a Hidalgo rodeado de esclavos encadenados.

LIBERTAD
REFORMA

(06-04) En la parte inferior (abajo) vemos a algunos de los líderes de las llamadas "Leyes de Reforma de 1857", encabezadas por Benito Juárez (de corbata roja con los colores de México) quien llegará a ser presidente de México cuarenta años después.

(06-05) Quizás el mural más impresionante que pintó Orozco en Palacio de Gobierno en la cabecera de la escalinata principal es su emotivo homenaje al Padre Hidalgo (siguiente página primera foto). Se le ve en colores vivos, agarrando audazmente su antorcha encendida mientras levanta su puño izquierdo como símbolo de fuerza. No cabe duda de que se dedica a la defensa de sus ideales políticos.

(06-06) A los pies del Padre Hidalgo (siguiente página segunda foto), observamos las batallas libradas contra las fuerzas oscuras que siempre han explotado a los pobres. Los enemigos de los pobres y oprimidos caen en las llamas del infierno.

(06-07) Orozco utiliza tonos grises y negros para dar énfasis a su tema. Se necesitan muchos puñales para eliminar a los malhechores de México (siguiente página primera foto).

(06-08) En contraste, en el Salón de Sesiones del Poder Legislativo se muestra otra imagen de Hidalgo. Es menos exaltado y hasta triste. Se dice que fue la última obra mural pintada por Orozco. Abajo se ve lo que se llama *El circo contemporáneo.*

(06-09) También incluye otras fuerzas que hacen daño a la sociedad y sus símbolos como la cruz, la esvástica y la hoz y el martillo (abajo). Aquí, Orozco no promueve ninguna ideología política.

(06-10) Orozco usa el rojo para enfatizar la maldad de Hitler y la bandera roja y el martillo y la hoz del comunismo.

« - » - « - » - « - »

ACTIVIDADES

1. Lee más acerca del Palacio de Gobierno en Guadalajara. https://es.wikipedia.org/wiki/Palacio_de_Gobierno_de_Jalisco
2. Lee más sobre el Padre Hidalgo. https://es.wikipedia.org/wiki/Miguel_Hidalgo_y_Costilla
3. Lee acerca de Benito Juárez. https://es.wikipedia.org/wiki/Benito_Ju%C3%A1rez

« - » - « - » - « - »

CAPÍTULO SEIS: PREGUNTAS

1. Describe el Palacio de Gobierno. (01) (02)
2. ¿Cuándo se abolió la esclavitud en México? ¿Quién firmó el decreto? (03)
3. ¿Quién fue el líder de las llamadas "Leyes de Reforma" de México? (04)
4. Describe el mural más impresionante del Palacio de Gobierno. (05)
5. ¿A quién vemos a los pies del Padre Hidalgo? (06)
6. Describe la apariencia de estas personas. (07)
7. ¿Cuál fue el último mural que pintó Orozco? (08)
8. ¿Cuáles son algunos de los símbolos usados en esta pintura? ¿Qué simbolizan? (09) (10)

« - » - « - » - « - »

CAPÍTULO SIETE
OROZCO EN EL "HOSPICIO CABAÑAS"

(Primera Parte)

(07-01) Durante los años 1938 y 1939, Orozco pintó cincuenta y tres frescos en el actual Instituto Cultural Cabañas de la ciudad de Guadalajara (abajo). Este edificio histórico fue construido a principios del siglo XIX por el obispo Juan Cruz Ruiz de Cabañas. Eligió al famoso arquitecto Manuel Tolsá para realizar los diseños de lo que sería conocido en el futuro como el Hospicio (Orfanato) Cabañas hasta el año 1980. Este enorme edificio tiene 23 patios, 106 cuartos y 465 arcos.

(07-02) Aquí el obispo estableció con éxito un taller para huérfanos y un refugio para ancianos y discapacitados. En la siguiente página primera foto, vemos a algunos de los niños jugando en la calle frente al edificio en el año 1920.

(07-03) Dado que el orfanato contiene algunos de los frescos más famosos de Orozco, se convirtió en un centro de arte y cultura con el nombre de "Instituto Cultural Cabañas". Finalmente, en el año 1997, la UNESCO lo declaró Patrimonio de la Humanidad. Cuando Orozco comenzó a pintar los murales en los muros y el techo, trató de mostrar objetivamente los aspectos positivos y negativos de las dos culturas de México: la indígena y la española (abajo segunda foto).

(07-04) En el detalle de abajo, Felipe II de España porta una cruz y una corona, simbolizando la llegada de los españoles al Nuevo Mundo.

(07-05) Orozco pintó las imágenes de dos españoles famosos — el escritor Miguel Cervantes (izquierda) y el famoso pintor El Greco. Están sentados en un muro que culmina en un arco con una ventana entre ellos (abajo).

(07-06) Ambos van vestidos como hombres de distinción. A continuación, vemos un primer plano de Cervantes, autor de la famosa novela Don Quijote, algunos dicen que es la novela más leída de todos los tiempos.

(07-07) El Greco (abajo) fue uno de los pintores más notables de España. Orozco muestra que cada una de estas dos figuras es representativa de una ruptura cultural que cada uno hizo en su época.

(07-08) Orozco pintó una de las primeras carabelas o barcos que trajeron a Colón y otros primeros exploradores al Nuevo Mundo (abajo). Colón creía que había llegado a las Indias Orientales, donde encontraría las especias que tenían mucha demanda en Europa. Por eso llamó indios a los nativos.

(07-09) La escena de la siguiente página (primera foto) un conquistador a lomos de un caballo de dos cabezas representa la conquista de México. Tenochtitlán, la capital azteca (ahora Ciudad de México) cayó en manos de los españoles en 1521. Los caballos jugaron un papel importante en la conquista, ya que los indígenas nunca antes habían visto este tipo de animal. Al principio, los nativos creían que el jinete y el caballo eran un solo animal. Los españoles los utilizaron como medio de transporte y, montados, pudieron matar a muchos indios.

(07-10) Según Orozco, los indios veían a los caballos como animales con cabezas de metal. A sus pies yacen algunas de las numerosas víctimas indígenas de este extraño animal (abajo segunda foto).

« - » - « - » - « - »

ACTIVIDADES

1. Lee sobre el obispo Juan Cruz Ruiz de Cabañas. https://es.wikipedia.org/wiki/Juan_Cruz_Ruiz_de_Caba%C3%B1as
2. Lee acerca del Instituto Cultural Cabañas. https://es.wikipedia.org/wiki/Hospicio_Caba%C3%B1as
3. Lee sobre Miguel de Cervantes. https://es.wikipedia.org/wiki/Miguel_de_Cervantes
4. Lee acerca de El Greco. https://es.wikipedia.org/wiki/El_Greco

« - » - « - » - « - »

CAPÍTULO SIETE: PREGUNTAS

1. ¿Cuántos frescos pintó Orozco en el Instituto Cultural Cabañas? (01)
2. ¿Quién construyó este edificio histórico? (01)
3. ¿Qué arquitecto eligió para el diseño? (01)
4. ¿Hasta qué año sirvió este edificio como orfanato? (01)
5. Describe este edificio. (01)
6. ¿Para qué sirvió este edificio? (02)
7. ¿Qué ocurrió en el año 1997? (03)
8. ¿Qué trató de mostrar Orozco en sus murales? (03)
9. Describe cómo retrata Orozco al rey Felipe II. (04)
10. ¿Qué dos españoles famosos pintó Orozco? (05)
11. Describe cómo Orozco colocó a estos dos españoles en el mural. (05)
12. ¿Qué famosa novela escribió Cervantes? (06)
13. ¿Quién es uno de los pintores más notables de España? (07)
14. ¿Qué tipo de barco se utilizó para llevar a Colón al Nuevo Mundo? (08)
15. ¿Por qué trató de encontrar Colón una nueva ruta a las Indias Orientales? (08)

16. ¿Cuál fue la importancia de los caballos en el Nuevo Mundo? (09)
17. ¿Cómo se llamaba la capital azteca? (09)
18. ¿Por qué, acaso, pinta Orozco un caballo de dos cabezas? (09)
19. ¿Cómo veían los indios a los caballos en esa época? (10)

« - » - « - » - « - »

CAPÍTULO OCHO
OROZCO EN EL "HOSPICIO CABAÑAS"

(Segunda Parte)

(08-01) Después de llegar a la Nueva España (México), los españoles quedaron horrorizados por los sacrificios humanos realizados por los indígenas. Con figuras e imágenes dinámicas, Orozco pintó estos rituales primitivos y sangrientos practicados por las culturas prehispánicas (abajo).

(08-02) El tema del mural (siguiente página primera foto) es la conquista armada como símbolo de la violencia. Aquí vemos a Cortés como una máquina. Su cuerpo se mantiene unido con tuercas, pernos y tornillos. En la parte superior del mural, Cortés parece tener su brazo mecánico protegiendo al sacerdote. Incluso su espada parece ser una extensión de su cuerpo. A sus pies están los cuerpos mutilados de indios. Como resultado, la espada de Cortés está manchada con la sangre de la raza indígena.

(08-03) Al mirar el mural al revés, podemos ver mejor el retrato del sacerdote. Tal vez esta sea la forma en que Orozco presenta a ambos como cómplices de la subyugación y muerte de tantos de la raza indígena (abajo).

(08-04) Por otro lado, Orozco retrató la caridad cristiana que los españoles trajeron al Nuevo Mundo. Un sacerdote reza por el alma de una víctima reciente que yace a sus pies (abajo).

(08-05) Orozco también critica las grandes luchas y conflictos que causaron la muerte de tantos españoles como de indios (abajo).

(08-06) En otro mural del Hospicio Cabañas, Orozco muestra cómo los curas intentaban convertir a los indígenas al catolicismo y enseñarles diferentes oficios. De hecho, después de la conquista, diferentes Órdenes Católicas construyeron cientos de conventos para enseñar el idioma español a los indios (Observa las letras ABCD). El cordón anudado que lleva el sacerdote abajo indica que es de la Orden Franciscana. Dado que la punta de la cruz se parece más a una daga, tal vez Orozco esté dando a entender que las conversiones no siempre se hicieron con el libre albedrío de los indios.

(08-07) La rueda, desconocida por los pueblos indígenas del Nuevo Mundo, simboliza los avances de la civilización occidental que luego dieron origen a la mecanización en la sociedad mexicana de esa época (siguiente página primera foto).

(08-08) Según Orozco, a medida que nuevos inventos como la rueda cambian el mundo, las personas tienden a olvidar las tradiciones y costumbres de sus antepasados. Abajo vemos que la rueda quizás ha aplastado a los viejos poetas y filósofos de los siglos pasados.

(08-09) El pintor también muestra el contraste entre los primeros rudimentos de la ciencia introducidos por los europeos y las supersticiones de las culturas indígenas de México (abajo a la derecha).

(08-10) En el detalle de la siguiente página primera foto, Orozco pinta a los demagogos, vestidos de negro, que se encuentran en todos los niveles de la sociedad mexicana.

(08-11) Otro cuadro muestra a un grupo de déspotas que aparecen con diferentes rostros en todos los colores (siguiente página segunda foto.

(08-12) En otro arco, Orozco pinta una estatua del querido obispo Juan Cruz de Cabañas quien, hace tantos años, fundó el orfanato para niños pobres desamparados y ancianos desamparados de Guadalajara (abajo).

(08-13) Muchos críticos dicen que el punto culminante del arte de Orozco es su fresco llamado *Hombre en llamas* (siguiente página) que se puede ver en la cúpula del Hospicio Cabañas. Tiene aproximadamente siete metros de diámetro y veinticuatro metros de alto. Este gigantesco mural circular está rodeado por otros dieciséis frescos más pequeños con diferentes temas relacionados con el *Hombre en Llamas*.

(08-14) En el mural circular podemos distinguir cuatro personas, una figura en el centro y otras tres entrelazadas alrededor de la primera. Hay varias interpretaciones del significado de esta obra maestra. Para algunos, el mural representa el mundo de las culturas indígenas y sus bárbaros sacrificios humanos. En el detalle siguiente, la figura del centro puede ser la persona sacrificada por las otras tres personas que le rodean (siguiente página primera foto). Quizás el hombre de la parte inferior sea el sacerdote encargado de realizar el sacrificio. Así, el color rojo no solo representa las llamas, sino también la sangre de la víctima. Otros sugieren que las figuras del mural representan los cuatro elementos de la naturaleza — fuego, aire, agua y tierra. Otra posible interpretación es que la figura en el centro es quizás Cristo que está siendo sacrificado por los pecados del Hombre. Puede ser que las imágenes más pequeñas alrededor de las cuatro personas representen pecados como la guerra, la esclavitud, la crueldad y otros males de la sociedad moderna.

(08-15) Otros críticos sostienen que la figura principal del fresco representa a Prometeo, el dios que entregó el fuego a la humanidad (siguiente página segunda foto). El hombre debajo de él puede ser Zeus. Es irónico que Prometeo esté siendo consumido por el mismo fuego que le dio a la humanidad. El efecto más importante del mural es que nos hace pensar. No es necesario tener un solo significado en mente para apreciar esta magnífica obra de Orozco.

« - » - « - » - « - »

ACTIVIDADES

1. Lee acerca de Prometeo.
   https://es.wikipedia.org/wiki/Prometeo
2. Lee sobre Zeus.
   https://es.wikipedia.org/wiki/Zeus

« - » - « - » - « - »

CAPÍTULO OCHO: PREGUNTAS

1. ¿Qué país es hoy la Nueva España? (01)
2. ¿Qué horrorizó a los españoles cuando llegaron a la Nueva España? (01)
3. ¿Cómo se representa a Cortés en uno de los frescos de Orozco? (02)
4. Describe el cuerpo de Cortés en ese fresco. (02)
5. ¿Quién está representado con Cortés en el mismo fresco? (03)
6. Describe cómo representa Orozco la caridad cristiana. (04)
7. ¿Qué crítica Orozco? (05)
8. ¿Qué hacían muchos sacerdotes españoles en la Nueva España? (06)
9. ¿Qué significan las letras ABCD en ese fresco? (06)
10. ¿Quién construyó cientos de conventos en la Nueva España? (06)
11. ¿Qué significa el cordón anudado? (06)
12. ¿Qué simboliza la rueda en otro de los frescos de Orozco? (07)
13. Según Orozco, ¿cómo cambia la rueda el mundo? (08)
14. ¿Qué contraste muestra Orozco en ese fresco? (09)
15. Describe cómo retrata Orozco a los demagogos. (10)
16. Describe cómo retrata Orozco a los déspotas. (11)
17. Describe la estatua del obispo Juan Cruz de Cabañas. (12)

18. Según muchos críticos, ¿cuál es el punto culminante del arte de Orozco? (13)
19. Describe ese fresco. (13)
20. Mencione las posibles interpretaciones de ese fresco. (14)
21. ¿Qué puede representar la figura principal de ese fresco para otros críticos? (15)

« - » - « - » - « - »

EXAMEN FINAL

Elija la mejor respuesta e indíquela con la letra correspondiente.

1. José Clemente Orozco nació en el Estado de
   (a) Nayarit
   (b) Mazatlán
   (c) Jalisco
   (d) Oaxaca

2. Cuando aún era joven, la familia de Orozco se mudó a
   (a) la Ciudad de México
   (b) Guadalajara
   (c) Monterrey
   (d) Oaxaca

3. El joven José (Orozco) quedó impresionado con el trabajo de un dibujante y grabador llamado
   (a) Diego Rivera
   (b) Dr. Atl
   (c) David Alfaro Siqueiros
   (d) José Guadalupe Posada

4. Después de la muerte de su padre, José comenzó a estudiar
   (a) agricultura
   (b) arte
   (c) ley
   (d) medicina

5. Durante un accidente con fuegos artificiales, los médicos se vieron en la necesidad de amputarle el (la)
   (a) pierna
   (b) brazo

(c) mano
(d) pie

6. Uno de los primeros trabajos de José como dibujante se titula *La casa de*
   (a) *alegría*
   (b) *miedo*
   (c) *terror*
   (d) *lágrimas*

7. Algunos críticos han comparado el arte de José en este momento con el de
   (a) Toulouse-Lautrec
   (b) El Greco
   (c) Rembrandt
   (d) Pablo Picasso

8. En el año 1922 asumió el cargo un nuevo Director de Educación Pública. Su nombre fue
   (a) José Vasconcelos
   (b) Diego Rivera
   (c) David Alfaro Siqueiros
   (d) José Guadalupe Posada

9. El nuevo Director de Educación Pública quería educar a las masas por medio de
   (a) visitas gratuitas al Palacio de Bellas Artes
   (b) visitas a museos de arte
   (c) arte pintado en los muros de edificios públicos
   (d) clases de arte gratuitas

10. Uno de los murales de Orozco se titula Cortés y
   (a) Felipe II
   (b) Malinche
   (c) Pizarro
   (d) Xicoténcatl

11. El mural de Orozco titulado *Banquete de ricos* muestra la riqueza de los ricos y
(a) el descontento de la clase baja
(b) sus hermosas casas
(c) las mejoras realizadas por la Revolución Mexicana
(d) la nueva Ciudad de México de esa época

12. Uno de los símbolos del comunismo es el (la)
(a) martillo
(b) hacha
(c) arado
(d) espada

13. En el año 1928, Orozco recibió una comisión del Pomona College para pintar un mural llamado
(a) *Poseidón*
(b) *Apolo*
(c) *Prometeo*
(d) *Zeus*

14. La Caja de Pandora contenía
(a) riquezas
(b) males
(c) cenizas
(d) muerte

15. Orozco luego pintó una serie de murales titulados *La epopeya de la civilización americana* en
(a) Knox College
(b) William & Mary College
(c) Bowdoin College
(d) Dartmouth College

16. En uno de los murales de la serie anterior, Orozco pinta un mítico dios blanco llamado
(a) Tláloc
(b) Quetzalcóatl

(c) Huitzilopochtli
(d) Tonatiuh

17. En el mismo cuadro se ve a Cortés de pie detrás de una cruz negra que representa la muerte de(l)
(a) hombre blanco
(b) España
(c) la civilización indígena de México
(d) Quetzalcóatl

18. Luego de terminar sus murales en Estados Unidos, Orozco acepta una invitación para pintar murales en la ciudad de
(a) Guadalajara
(b) Monterrey
(c) Oaxaca
(d) Puebla

19. En estos murales, uno de los temas principales es la Revolución Mexicana que tuvo lugar entre 1910 y
(a) 1915
(b) 1920
(c) 1925
(d) 1930

20. En la antigua Roma, los aspirantes a cargos públicos usaban togas, ¿de qué color?
(a) blanco
(b) negro
(c) rojo
(d) azul

21. La capital del Estado de Jalisco es
(a) Monterrey
(b) Oaxaca
(c) Puebla
(d) Guadalajara

22. El líder que firmó el decreto de abolición de la esclavitud en México fue
(a) Miguel Hidalgo
(b) Porfirio Díaz
(c) Pancho Villa
(d) Emiliano Zapata

23. El Instituto Cultural Cabañas fue originalmente un(a)
(a) iglesia
(b) orfanato
(c) prisión
(d) convento

24. En el techo del Instituto Cultural Cabañas, Orozco pintó
(a) un caballo con dos cabezas
(b) dos pintores franceses
(c) el rey Carlos I
(d) el hombre "pentafásico"

25. Muchos críticos dicen que el punto culminante del arte de Orozco es su fresco llamado
(a) *El hombre al volante*
(b) *El hombre en llamas*
(c) *El hombre en la encrucijada*
(d) *El hombre en guerra*

« - » - « - » - « - »

ACERCA DEL AUTOR

El Dr. Harry E. Babbitt es un ciudadano norteamericano que durante 42 años fue profesor de español en escuelas secundarias y universidades. Al mismo tiempo, ha sido y es un meticuloso investigador de la cultura hispanoamericana, lo que le llevó a realizar docenas de viajes por España y América Latina para ampliar sus investigaciones y complementarlas con películas, videos y fotografías. Como resultado de esta amplia experiencia, ahora está publicando guías bilingües de nivel intermedio, para que los estudiantes puedan practicar su idioma de destino y al mismo tiempo aprender sobre la extensa y diversa cultura de España y América Latina.

TAMBIÉN DISPONIBLES EN AMAZON

ESTUDIOS ESPAÑOLES Y LATINOAMERICANOS

(LO DIFÍCIL HECHO FÁCIL)

Recomendados para estudiantes de la secundaria y universidad como introducción al estudio de obras maestras culturales y literarias.

TÍTULOS DISPONIBLES
EDICIÓN BILINGÜE
"Libros" & "Kindle eBooks"
(Buscar en libros: "Harry E. Babbitt Ph. D.", incluídos los siguientes):

HISTORIA DE ESPAÑA

El Viejo Camino de Santiago en España
Historia de Moros y Cristianos en España
El Camino de Santiago en España
El Camino de Santiago en Francia
La Batalla de Navas de Tolosa
La Batalla de Covadonga
La Batalla de Guadalete
La España Prerromana
La España Visigoda
La España Islámica
La España Romana

LITERATURA DE ESPAÑA

Don Quijote de la Mancha P1 Comentado y Resumido
La vida de Lazarillo de Tormes y de sus fortunas y adversidades
Llanto por Ignacio Sánchez Mejías Comentado
Sor Juana Inés de la Cruz: la Décima Musa
Gustavo Adolfo Bécquer Rimas y Leyendas
La Tierra de Alvargonzález Comentada

La Casa de Bernarda Alba Comentada
San Manuel Bueno, Mártir Comentado
La Celestina Comentada y Abreviada
Breve Historia de la Lengua Española
Dime qué lees y Te diré quién eres Comentado
La Zapatera Prodigiosa Comentada
Antonio Machado: Poeta de Soria
El Cantar del Mío Cid Comentado
Romancero Gitano Comentado
Bodas de Sangre Comentada
Don Juan Tenorio Comentado
El Viejo Romancero Español
Poema de Fernán González
Mariana Pineda Comentado
Fuente Ovejuna Comentado
Yerma Comentada

ARTE DE ESPAÑA

Salvador Dalí y el Torero Alucinógeno
Arte e Historia de la Tauromaquia (Corrida de Toros)
Diego Velázquez y su España
El Arte Románico en España
Francisco Goya y su España
Pablo Picasso y su España
El Guernica de Picasso
El Greco y su España

AMERICA: DESCUBRIMIENTO Y CONQUISTA

La Historia Verdadera de la Conquista de la Nueva España
Vasco Núñez de Balboa descubre el Océano Pacifico
Fray Bernardino de Sahagún Misionero e Historiador
Fernando Magallanes Descubridor Extraordinario
Cristóbal Colon Almirante del Mar Océano
Francisco Pizarro y la Conquista del Perú

HARRY E BABBITT
JOSÉ CLEMENTE OROZCO MEXICAN MURALIST
JOSÉ CLEMENTE OROZCO MURALISTA MEXICANO

Hernán Cortés y la Conquista de México

HISTORIA LATINOAMERICANA

Bartolomé de las Casas: Protector de los Indios
Miguel Hidalgo y la Independencia de México
Inca Garcilaso de la Vega: Comentador Real
José de San Martín: Libertador Argentino
Simón Bolívar: Libertador Venezolano
Seis Culturas Antiguas de México
José Martí Patriota Cubano

LITERATURA LATINOAMERICANA

La Vuelta de Martin Fierro: Fragmentos Comentado
Domingo Faustino Sarmiento y su Facundo
La Araucana: Fragmentos Comentada
Martin Fierro: Fragmentos Comentado
Gabriela Mistral Poeta de Chile
Pablo Neruda en sus Palabras
Pablo Neruda Poeta de Chile
Rubén Darío: El Modernismo
El Popol Vuh

ARTE LATINOAMERICANO

Diego Rivera: Murales en el Palacio Nacional P1
Diego Rivera: Murales en el Palacio Nacional P2
La Herencia Española en los Estados Unidos
El Subte de Buenos Aires: su Historia y Arte
David Alfaro Siqueiros Muralista Mexicano
Conventos Mexicanos del Siglo XVI
El Día de los Muertos en México
Cementerios de Buenos Aires

PARA UN LISTADO COMPLETO
O PARA MÁS INFORMACIÓN
ESCRIBIR A:
quiquesatx@gmail.com

Printed in Great Britain
by Amazon

35455790R00096